How to Build
Supercharged & Turbocharged
Small-Block Fords

BOB McCLURG

CarTech
Auto Books & Manuals

Edited by: Travis Thompson
Designed by: Christopher Fayers

ISBN-13 978-1-884089-96-1
ISBN-10 1-884089-96-8

Order No. SA95

Printed in China

CarTech®, Inc.,
39966 Grand Avenue
North Branch, MN 55056
Telephone (651) 277-1200 • (800) 551-4754 • Fax: (651) 277-1203
www.cartechbooks.com

OVERSEAS DISTRIBUTION BY:

Brooklands Books Ltd.
P.O. Box 146, Cobham, Surrey, KT11 1LG, England
Telephone 01932 865051 • Fax 01932 868803
www.brooklands-books.com

Brooklands Books Aus.
3/37-39 Green Street, Banksmeadow, NSW 2109, Australia
Telephone 2 9695 7055 • Fax 2 9695 7355

Cover and Cover Inset:
Your supercharged or turbocharged engine may not start to be this serious, but it's important to understand how the whole system works together. The Mustang in the main cover image features a Roots-style blower, while the fuel-injected engine in the inset photo features a pair of turbochargers. Your engine doesn't have to be as shiny as these to run well.

Title Page:
The Hellion Power Systems air-to-air intercooler is secured to the 2000 Mustang front radiator support bulkhead using a pair of metric bolts. Air-to-air intercoolers like this are used in centrifugal supercharges as well as turbochargers.

Back Cover Top:
Now it's time to install the 2.2L Kenne Bell Blowzilla twin-screw supercharger onto the GT40 lower intake. As you can see, this is a two-man job.

Back Cover Lower Left:
Once the centrifugal supercharger is installed, you can move on to the driver's side supercharger air intake duct and K&N conical air filter assembly.

Back Cover Lower Right:
Put the turbocharger in place and bolt it up to the turbocharger support bracket using a series of three ½ x ⁵⁄₁₆-inch bolts.

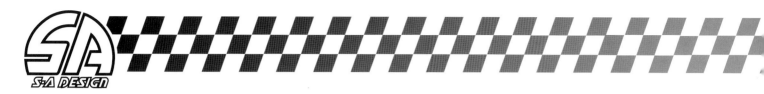

Dedication

This book is dedicated to the memory of Gladys Louise McClurg, who encouraged her son to pursue the things that interested him in life, and follow his heart.

ABOUT THE AUTHOR

By his own admission, automotive journalist Bob McClurg has been a "car guy" ever since he was old enough to realize what one was. "When I was about eight or nine, I remember intently watching my father, Bob Sr., rebuild a 1941 Ford Flathead V-8 on the floor of our family garage. I knew right then and there that I wanted to become more involved with cars!"

Of course, school came first, and it was there where Bob eventually realized he had a knack for putting his thoughts into words. Eventually, his writing and love for cars would come together. "I was probably the only kid on the block to have my own subscription to *Hot Rod* magazine. Once a month, my world would come to a screeching halt the minute my monthly copy of *Hot Rod* arrived in the mail. It didn't take long for me to realize that that was *exactly* what I wanted to do for the rest of my life."

The prolific journalist's 40-year automotive portfolio reads like a magazine industry who's-who list, including *Hot Rod* magazine (Bob was *HRM*'s photo editor from 1977 to 1979), *Car Craft* magazine, *Super Stock & Drag Illustrated* (McClurg was *SS&DI*'s photo editor in 1969), *Popular Hot Rodding, Kit Car, Super Chevy, Muscle Mustangs & Fast Fords, Drag Racer, Chevy Rumble, Super Rod, Street Trucks, Street Rodder, Rod & Custom, Truckin', Ford Builder*, and countless other automotive enthusiast titles.

In spite of covering just about any subject having to do with hot rodding, McClurg is best known for two things:

his early 1960s to late 1970s drag racing lens work, which was featured in CarTech's recent release, *Dragsters, Funnies, Gassers & Altereds: Drag Racing's Golden Age*, and his love for Fords, specifically the Mustang.

As the former editor of both *Mustang Illustrated* and *Ford High Performance* magazines, Bob's Ford knowledge led him to author three books on the subject, including *Classics in Colour #6 Mustang, Mustang, the Next Generation*, and *Mustang, Selling the Legend*.

His latest CarTech title, *How to Build Supercharged and Turbocharged Small-Block Fords* draws extensively from Bob's automotive background. "I've always loved blown cars, no matter what kind," says Bob. Take a look at Bob's collection of special interest Fords, you'll realize that's no idle boast. McClurg owns no less than four blown street cars, including a one-of-one, PowerDyne-supercharged '98 Saleen XP/8 Mercury Mountaineer test vehicle. "It's like driving a four-door 5.0L Mustang GT," says McClurg. Also on Bob's equipment roster is the former *Mustang Illustrated* Vortech-supercharged '89 Mustang GT known as *Ground Zero*, and a '65 Mustang convertible with a Kenne-Bell-supercharged 5.0L, known as the *Skunk*, featured elsewhere in this book.

Bob McClurg is also a member of the Society of Automotive Engineers (SAE), as well as a member of one of the oldest extant car enthusiast clubs in the western United States, the *Road Kings* of Burbank, California.

INTRODUCTION

Superchargers and turbochargers have both been around for over a century. What makes them so popular? Looks, power, performance, sound, and status. And how do they relate to small-block Ford engines? That's exactly what this book is all about!

The modern supercharger, whether it's a traditional Roots type, a compact scroll-type centrifugal supercharger, or a relatively new "screw type" blower, started life as nothing more than an air pump.

Roots Blowers

Of the three designs, the Roots blower is by far the most popular in the world. It was originally designed in 1854 by Francis and Philander Roots in an attempt to improve the efficiency of the power system in their woolen mill in Connersville, Indiana. The brothers designed a "water wheel" made out of wood, but the device warped and jammed when exposed to moisture. Quite by accident, the brothers discovered that their pump moved air far easier (and with fewer problems) than it moved water. They improved on their basic design, creating the rotary positive displacement blower in the process.

The Roots low-pressure blower consisted of a pair of twisted rotors spinning inside a case. Cool, dense air was drawn through the inlet in the top of the case, then around and through the twin rotors, which were powered by chains or belts. The compressed air was then discharged out the bottom of the case. By the 1890s, the Roots blower

Roots blowers are the classic superchargers that most people think of sticking up through the hood with a pair of big carbs. Many types of modern superchargers fit under the stock hood.

was widely used to deliver fresh air to coal mines.

In 1893, a Roots engineer broke away from the parent company and founded the Connersville Blower Company. The two entities continued as bitter trade rivals until the International Derrick and Equipment Company (IDECO) purchased and merged both firms in 1931.

By then the patent had expired and the Roots blower design had become public domain. Once the automotive sector got its hands on it, things changed

but quick! When a Roots blower was used with combustible fuels like diesel, gasoline, alcohol, or (much later) mixes of alcohol and nitromethane fuels, the result was a denser, more compressed air/fuel intake charge that significantly increased horsepower.

Mercedes was probably the first automotive manufacturer to adapt the Roots twin-rotor compressor design to the automobile. They began development in 1919, and in 1926 introduced the supercharged K model. At the time, it

When you take an already powerful V-8 engine and add a supercharger, you're going to need extra air and fuel. This is why it's so common to see supercharged engines running two carbs instead of one.

Nothing gets attention like a polished supercharger sticking up through the hood. Supercharged engines look good, sound great, and run even better.

was used on his famous front-wheel-drive "Coffin Nose" Cords, with Indianapolis 500 great Harry Miller serving as project engineer. Not surprisingly, Cord's creations were some of the fastest road cars in their day.

But how did the Roots blower come to be commonly referred to (in the hot-rod world, anyway) as the GMC blower? The name was popularized through product use on GMC-manufactured buses built from the early 1940s to the late 1970s, and these blowers were rated according to engine size.

For example, if you had an inline two-cylinder diesel engine with a displacement of 71ci per cylinder (a standard GM diesel bore size), the blower would have been referred to as a "2-71." If the engine was a four-cylinder inline diesel engine with 71ci per cylinder, the designation would be "4-71," and a six-cylinder inline diesel engine would likewise be designated as a "6-71."

Legend has it that hot rodders first experimented with the GMC blower at the Bonneville Salt Flats in the late 1940s, where altitude and air density affect performance. Although there is some question as to exactly who was the very first salt flats racer to run a supercharger (a term reportedly coined by hot rodders), the names Tom Beatty, Don Blair, and Chuck Potvin (the latter of which would actually go on to build his own crank-driven blower kits) most often come up in conversations.

The late Mickey Thompson and U.S. Nationals Top Eliminator winner Calvin Rice (with engine builder Doug Hartelts) were some of the first drag racers to experiment with a GMC supercharger.

Rice and Hartelts *Hot Rod Magazine Special* established a flying kilometer record at March Air Force Base in 1958 running a blown Chrysler Hemi. Of course, other well-known drag racers like "Big Daddy" Don Garlits, Art and Jack Chrisman, Chris "the Greek" Karamesines, Connie Kalitta, and others followed.

Probably the greatest and most significant technical innovation in supercharging history occurred in the early 1960s when Cragar Equipment (a division of Bell Auto Parts) and the Mickey Thompson Equipment Company (M/T)

was the fastest production car in the world, with a top speed of 145 mph.

Closer to home, Detroit Diesel introduced the design at the 1928 World's Fair. Detroit Diesel engineers used the scavenging principles of the Roots air pump to increase overall volumetric efficiency and enhance cylinder combustion using the era's low-octane diesel fuels.

With the 1931 release of the Roots-manufactured centrifugal (automotive) compressor, the design went mainstream. One of the first to give it a whirl (1937) was E. L. Cord. The Roots design

Centrifugal superchargers have gained huge popularity with the late-model Mustang crowd. They fit under the stock hood and require a minimum of modifications to be effective.

individually pioneered the cog belt blower drive, eliminating that dangerously nasty chain drive system.

The considerably safer cog belt blower drive also allowed racers to experiment with various size blower drive pulleys to come up with different drive ratio pulley combinations.

But where does the GMC-derived, street blower segment of the supercharger aftermarket come in? Although blown street cars have been around as long as their drag racing counterparts, the supercharger setups weren't usually too far off from race-only setups. Of course, this accounted for a rather unmanageable street machine. However, by the late 1970s, companies like Dyers Blower Service, Weiand, and Blower Drive Service (BDS) "civilized" the breed by engineering kits with all the accessory drive brackets and components.

Centrifugal Blowers

While the GMC or Roots-type street superchargers are big sellers with the fat-tire, Pro/Street segment of the sport, the relatively compact centrifugal or "scroll-type" street supercharger is as big a seller with the OE segment because of their compact size.

Robert Paxton McCulloch designed the first gear-driven centrifugal blower for the popular Ford Flathead engine in 1937. The McCulloch Centrifugal Supercharger possessed a maximum boost level of 4 psi, and its impeller was driven by a set of worm gears that received its lubrication from the engine crankcase.

Although McCulloch's gear-drive blower was lauded by everyone from Indianapolis to Southern California's dry lakes, it was noisy and generally dismissed as impractical for OE street applications. Then World War II came along.

Submarines were widely used by the Navy in World War II, but ventilation proved a major problem during lengthy subsurface runs. McCulloch applied the basic engineering principles of the two-stage blower from 1937 along with the development of a quieter reciprocating ball-bearing drive. McCulloch was awarded a U.S. Navy contract to produce his "silent running" air pumps.

When thousands of GI's returned home after the war (some with hot rods in storage), McCulloch recognized a ready and waiting street supercharger market.

Combining the best design features of his air pump, and about $700,000 in research money, McCulloch designed the two-stage McCulloch VS-57, released in 1953. The McCulloch VS-57 supercharger utilized a planetary ball bearing drive that offered a 4.4:1 step-up ratio from its input shaft to the impeller. Rather than rely on lubrication from the engine, the VS-57 was self-lubricating via a mechanical oil pump and reservoir using automatic transmission fluid.

McCulloch's VS-57 offered a maximum boost of 5 psi, and excellent bottom end operating characteristics. Boost was controlled using a variable rate input pulley driven by a v-belt. This system allowed the pulley speed (and therefore the boost level) to change based on engine RPM and accessory power loads. McCulloch's produced close to 46,000 VS-57 centrifugal superchargers; it was so popular it was used on '50s production cars like the Kaiser Manhattan, the Studebaker Golden Hawk, the Packard Clipper, and the Packard Hawk.

In 1956, McCulloch set up a special automotive division known as Paxton Products, and developed a new supercharger. The VR-57 featured a variable-rate internal planetary drive ratio capable of altering the step-up ratio from 3.5:1 to 5.5:1. This variable rate was achieved by a spring pack that changed the distance between ball races based on engine RPM.

The new Paxton VR-57 was so good that after being briefly used by the Ford teams in NASCAR competition, it was outlawed. On the street side of the coin, the VR-57's most notable claim to fame was its use on the 1957 Ford Thunderbirds (a.k.a. Blower Birds), of which 211 were produced.

In 1958, Andy Granatelli set numerous land speed records at Bonneville driving a Paxton SN-60-equipped Studebaker Hawk. Realizing a good thing when they saw it, the Granatelli brothers (Andy, Joe, and Vince) eventually bought Paxton.

A few years later, the Paxton name would again be back in the limelight after Carroll Shelby teamed up with Paxton, first on a Paxton-supercharged 289 Cobra, later a 427 model, and then on a Paxton-supercharged 1966 Shelby GT-350 Mustang. These Mustangs were produced in limited quantity from 1966 to 1968, and this setup was also made available as an over-the-counter-option on small-block Mustang models produced from 1965 to 1972.

However, in the early 1970s, the fuel crisis and rising energy costs threatened the automotive industry. Paxton focused on other markets (including the military), yet continued to sell its SN-60 blower and service components.

Then in 1979, Ford released its all-new Fox Platform aero Mustang, and everything changed. Paxton immediately responded with the compact SN-60-based street supercharger kit for the carbureted 5.0L (302-cid) Ford small-block. However, carburetors were somewhat limited by the amount of boost (5 to 6 psi) they could take. Thankfully, Ford introduced the Sequential Electronic Fuel Injection (SEFI) system for the 5.0L Mustang and 5.0L-equipped Ford passenger cars in 1986. Paxton introduced an updated version of the SN-60 known as the SN-89, and became the first aftermarket manufacturer to come out with a 50-state-emissions-legal street supercharger kit.

In essence, the Fox Mustang and the Paxton SN-89 (later updated to the SN-92, SN-93, and SN-95 versions) basically wrote their own chapter on emissions-legal street supercharging.

Of course, other manufacturers like Vortech Engineering, ATI-Pro Charger, and PowerDyne Products released their own scroll-type, centrifugal street superchargers, and we'll discuss them at length in Chapter 3.

Twin-Screw Blowers

The third most commonly recognized street supercharger is the twin-screw supercharger, invented by Swedish engineer Alf Lysholm in 1936.

Over the years, the Lysholm design has been applied to numerous automotive applications throughout the world.

This polished Kenne Bell twin-screw supercharger sits atop a 32-valve 4.6-liter engine. Twin-screw blowers are more efficient than traditional Roots-style superchargers.

Centrifugal superchargers are more efficient at high RPM where some engines, like this 32-valve 4.6-liter Cobra engine, make their power. At 7,000 rpm, a standard Roots blower would probably be out of its efficiency range and just be beating hot air.

Screw blower technology in the U.S. was introduced sometime in the 1980s to professional drag racing by former top fuel and funny car racer Art Whipple. This design was later adapted to the street by companies like Whipple Supercharger Systems and Kenne Bell Superchargers.

Turbocharging

When it comes to turbochargers, the basic theory of pumping air into an engine to increase its volumetric efficiency and enhance performance is the same. However, the applied principle is very different.

The turbocharger concept was first developed in Switzerland in 1912, and saw limited use on aircraft in World War I.

By World War II, turbocharging had come into its own, and thousands were used on high altitude bombers like the B-17 Flying Fortress, the B-24 Liberator, and fighters like the P-38 and the P-

47. After the war, turbos were successful in marine, industrial, and diesel applications . . . but the company that popularized the turbocharger was Caterpillar, when they began experimenting with turbochargers in the early 1950s. However, they certainly wouldn't have done so without the help of a small heat exchanger manufacturer in Los Angeles, California, named "Garrett."

Because of their work with heat exchangers, Garrett had the facilities to test Caterpillar's in-house turbocharger, which failed miserably. Caterpillar wisely elected to subcontract all future turbocharger development and production to the small L.A. firm because of their heat exchanger experience. Ironically, one of the members on the Garrett team was a gentleman named Hugh McInnes who would go on to cast a tall shadow in the turbo-charging arena.

Garrett's first production turbo for Caterpillar was designated the T-15, and Caterpillar was so pleased it

ordered 5,000 of these small turbos for the famous D-9 bulldozer. As a result, the AiResearch Industrial Division of Garrett AiResearch was established in 1954 – the first corporation solely dedicated to the design and manufacture of turbochargers.

By the 1960s, AiResearch established itself as the undisputed industry leader, with a complete line of commercial turbocharger applications.

In the automotive sector, the first OE turbocharger application was the short-lived 1962 Oldsmobile Jetfire, powered by a 215-cid Oldsmobile aluminum V-8 engine equipped with a Garrett-AiResearch T-5 turbocharger. Unfortunately in those days, fuel-system technology and development was light-years away, and the high-compression, under-carbureted, water-and-alcohol injection system used on the Jetfire proved to be an exercise in engineering futility.

In 1965, GM also introduced the turbocharged Chevrolet Corvair Corsa

Turbochargers are currently the underdog in the high-performance aftermarket. The extra exhaust work that they require, and packaging issues, price most kits above the average supercharger kit. They do make amazing power though.

model, outfitted with a considerably more refined TRW-manufactured turbocharger system. Today, these cars are highly prized by collectors and in their time proved the viability of a mass-produced gasoline-burning turbocharged street car.

During the 1960s, many in the automotive aftermarket experimented with and perfected competition and street turbocharger systems. That included Ak Miller and his turbocharged dry lakes Fords. Also highly visible in the arena was Crown Manufacturing and its turbocharged Volkswagen and Corvair-powered dune buggies. Crane Cams, Fuel Injection Engineering (a.k.a. Hilborn Fuel Injection), along with Bob Keller and Hugh McInnes from a company called "Turbonics," were offering street turbochargers.

By the late 1960s, Rajay came onto the scene after purchasing the TRW turbocharger program, and hired Hugh McInnes away as Chief Engineer. One of the things that set it apart was that its products were made available at the grassroots level of the industry, in addition to the OE market.

These growing enterprises received a major boost in 1976 when Echlin Corporation created the Accel Turbosonic product line. Accel was able to educate the American public about the benefits of street turbocharging, and even acquired a company called Roto-Master to manufacture its own brand turbochargers.

In the late 1970s, Detroit enthusiastically rediscovered turbocharging. The threat of the fuel crisis of 1980, and government-imposed Corporate Average Fuel Economy (CAFE) standards, forced Detroit car manufacturers to revert to small-displacement "econoboxes" that may have delivered the required fuel numbers, but were grossly underpowered. With a turbocharger, some semblance of performance was restored; by the 1980s, virtually every automotive manufacturer in the world offered turbocharged engines.

Of course, many of today's modern imports offer turbocharged power trains, as do many domestic auto manufacturers, albeit to a lesser extent.

But where does that leave the automotive aftermarket? New breeds of aftermarket turbocharger companies and suppliers have sprung up, like HKS, Greddy, and Spearco-Turbonetics. They offer street turbo kits and/or related components.

Acknowledgments

The author thanks Kevin Boales, former editor of *Fabulous Mustangs* Magazine, for his technical support, research, writings, and keen interest in this project. Boales was extremely instrumental in helping out with the hard-core technical segments of this book, and created many of the charts and graphs.

Both author and publisher would also like to thank Craig Railsback, Blower Drive Service; Mr. Chas Night, Crane Cams; Matthew Held, Holley/Weiand; Jim Bell, Kenne Bell Superchargers; Jerry Magnuson, Magnuson Superchargers; Jim Wheeler, PowerDyne; Fred Piluso and Jeff Litnoff, Personal Touch Computers; Jim Middlebrook, Ricky Best, and Gil Cormase, Vortech Engineering; for their immense technical support and help on this project.

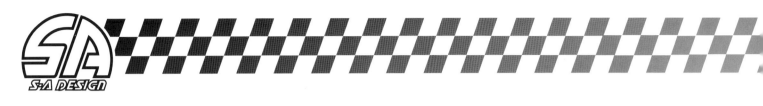

GENERAL CONSIDERATIONS FOR SUPERCHARGED ENGINES

Regardless of the type of supercharger you use, there are certain operating parameters that must be considered for your setup to work properly. Among them are particulars for each type of supercharger used – those will be detailed in individual chapters of this book dedicated to each 'charger type. However, the more general factors for a successful installation will be discussed here. These general considerations include:

• Increased intake airflow requirement
• Fuel system flow capability
• Ignition alterations, including timing, spark intensity, spark plug and wire selection
• Charge cooling (when used)
• Increased exhaust airflow and temperature
• Under-hood temperature considerations
• Cooling system requirements and upgrades

Intake Airflow

The basic idea behind supercharging is to make the engine think it's bigger than it really is. If we agree to dispense with the engineering math and finicky stuff for a moment, let's assume we're talking about a 302-ci engine, and an unnamed, general supercharger setup that can build as much as 15 pounds of positive manifold pres-

When you add a supercharger to your engine, you'll be making more horsepower, so it makes sense that you'll need more air and more fuel. This is one reason why Roots blowers are often topped with a pair of carburetors and a big air cleaner.

sure, or boost. Also assume the engine will take that boost and make good use of it without turning into a warhead.

On a theoretical average day, the static air pressure is 14.7 psi – against every surface that isn't in motion, and above an equally theoretical "zero"

point. In reality, the static air pressure around us varies considerably with altitude and the amount of moisture; an increase in either (or both) will cause a reduction in the atmospheric pressure.

For our example, though, let's presume we have a day that fits this average description. If anything causes pressure to fall significantly below the ambient pressure, it causes a vacuum. Think about how it feels to put your hand over the end of an idling engine's intake tube – as the engine runs, it will leave a formidable hickey on your palm before the engine stalls from lack of air. You're creating a pressure difference between the ambient air and the lower pressure inside the inlet pipe, which is why it sucks your hand in. The ambient air is merely attempting to regain its equal influence against every surface, everywhere.

Incidentally, an idling V-8 only creates a couple of pounds of negative differential pressure at its inlet. If it were more (let's say 20 psi of vacuum), it would easily break your hand into soft mushy stuff. That's enough meteorology for now.

When you're talking about boost, a static air pressure of 14.7 psi is usually called an atmosphere. You'll hear that term used when the conversation turns to boost pressure. For example, if a supercharged engine's manifold pressure rises to about 7.3 psi above ambient pressure, the engine is said to be running "half an atmosphere of boost." If the engine and supercharger can operate together well enough to bring the manifold pressure up to 14.7 psi, it's making one atmosphere of boost. That figure is rarely seen on the street, but it's completely reasonable for most race engines designed for supercharged operation. The difference there is primarily in the materials used to build the engine, and its architecture.

Now we get to the airflow part of our 302-ci scenario. A fresh small-block Ford consumes roughly 80 percent of its displacement volume for every two revolutions (720 degrees) of its crankshaft. It takes two revolutions to cycle all of the cylinders in a four-stroke, whether it's a five-horse Briggs & Stratton or one of John Force's fuel-burning Mustang funny cars.

The 80 percent factor is the volumetric efficiency (VE) of the engine, or the amount of air that is actually moved through the engine versus its total displacement. That's a fairly reasonable VE figure for a modern engine, but it's about

Just because a centrifugal blower is physically smaller than a Roots, doesn't mean it requires less air or fuel. With a modern fuel-injection system, you may need a set of larger injectors, a higher-flowing fuel pump, and an open-element air filter.

10 percent high for older engines with less computer time invested in optimizing their airflow characteristics. A naturally aspirated engine relies on the ambient air pressure to refill the cylinders with a fresh intake charge. The more efficient an engine is, the more it will take in while the intake valve is open, the higher the VE will be. With the addition of a supercharger, the VE will reach and exceed 100 percent as the manifold pressure goes positive (boost), regardless of engine RPM. Basically, with boost, you can stuff 10 lbs of crap in a 5 lb bag.

There can be occasional exceptions to this statement. If the intake tract is tragically wrong in its engineering, it won't matter how high the manifold pressure gets, you won't be able to get enough airflow to the cylinder heads. Amazingly enough, this has happened more than you might imagine, thanks to improperly matched airflow upgrades with an over-ambitious supercharger selection. In every case, the owner will have a look of disbelief on his face as the boost continues to rise, but the power output, well – doesn't.

In our example, the un-blown 302 manages to ingest, mix, burn, and get rid of about 400 cubic feet of air per minute (cfm) at 5,500 rpm, presuming its opera-

tor is not pussy-footing around and has the throttle wide open.

At that same 5,500 rpm, but with a supercharger installed and providing half an atmosphere (about 7 psi) of boost, the engine will be processing air at the rate of about 600 cfm. In effect, we've now tricked the engine into thinking it displaces 450 ci. It's dealing with the airflow of an engine that big, and if we did everything right, it'll make power like an engine of that size.

If we crank the boost up to a full atmosphere (about 15 psi), the engine will behave very much like it displaces 604 ci by processing more than 810 cfm of air at 5,500 rpm. That would be a formidable 302, indeed.

Those airflow figures are conservative because of another, less obvious, engine characteristic. A supercharger not only supplies the amount of air an engine uses under normal (non-supercharged) conditions, it also fills the internal volumes that can't be displaced by piston movement. Those areas include the combustion chamber volume above the pistons, which can be considerable, depending on the engine's cylinder head design, and also the entire intake manifold.

Fords have relatively compact combustion chambers in the interest of keeping the flame travel distance short, which help control emissions. Luckily, that compact volume provides a benefit when supercharging, because it reduces the distance the flame-front must travel after ignition, contributing to faster combustion and better control of the chamber temperature – which definitely goes up under boost, regardless of the chamber shape.

This all comes together when you decide how much boost you'll be using with your engine. The intake tract includes everything – each inch of tubing and all the bends, meanders, metering devices, sensor tips, screens, filters, and duct surfaces – between the combustion chamber and the air surrounding the car.

The intake tract must be capable of easily handling the airflow increase after a supercharger installation. If you plan to run more than a pound or two of boost, you'll need to loosen things up a bit along that twisted path, or the engine will never give you the results you want.

Horsepower is simply a figure that suggests how many times per time-unit an engine can produce a given amount of torque. It's calculated by multiplying torque by engine RPM, and then dividing it by a peculiarly interesting number: 5,252. Not exactly by coincidence, in the case of 4-cycle engines, 5,252 is the point on a horsepower/torque plot where the two lines converge – every time. This universal truth may have never jumped off a page at you before, but if the lines on your dyno chart don't meet at 5,252 rpm, someone made a mistake in the math.

This relationship is important because superchargers bring about a major change in torque curves versus a naturally aspirated engine. Once a blown engine establishes and begins maintaining a constant boost level in the manifold, the engine's torque curve flattens out and stays at that point for any higher RPM, unless the engine's airflow cannot keep up for some reason.

That's amazing news, especially if the blower can make good boost down low in the RPM range and keep up the good work as the engine speed climbs. As the RPM increases, the amount of air

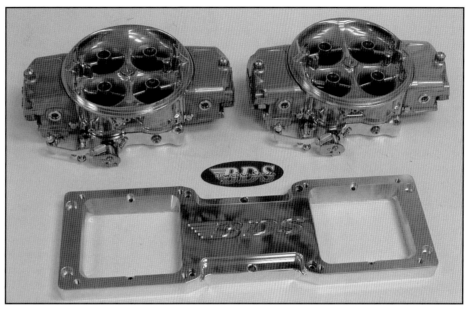

Most Roots blowers have room for two 4-bbls on top. You'll need to figure out how much power you're going to make, and then choose carbs accordingly. Having the right amount of air and fuel will literally make or break your supercharged engine.

it processes will climb accordingly, so it's logical that the blower must keep pace with the demand.

This function is easily seen at work if the needs of the entire system are not taken seriously. If the manifold pressure rises and stays put, but the torque curve then begins to sag, especially as it approaches 5,252 rpm, it means the airflow is being restricted somewhere between the air filter and the exhaust tips. Usually, the problem is in one of five areas listed below, beginning with the most important:

More blower speed than the engine can tolerate

Restrictive exhaust system

Inadequate intake manifold volume or flow rate

Very poor cam choice

Gasket mismatch at cylinder head ports

The accompanying plots reveal how torque and horsepower numbers relate to one another, and the difference a properly tuned supercharger will bring about in useful work from the engine. They also show how the area "under the curve" changes for the better – that's the improvement that should make you want to start saving for a blower kit.

Model-for-model intake tract modifications are detailed in later chapters because they're usually specific to the

type of supercharger used, its inlet configuration, intake manifold requirements, and packaging considerations.

Fuel System

If there's more air, you need more fuel. The stock fuel system may not have the ability to keep up with the demand of your supercharged 302. If your engine happens to be carbureted with a blow-through (supercharger blows through the carb) supercharger installation, the stock carb will usually be inadequate in both airflow and fuel-handling capabilities, even with very modest boost.

On the other hand, Fords with electronic fuel injection (EFI) of any kind – even TBI – can be made to work in most cases. If your engine is equipped with SEFI (Sequential Electronic Fuel Injection), you can really optimize the setup and reap the benefits of a fine-running supercharged engine.

Let's cover the carburetor situation first. When Shelby Cars decided on a Paxton blow-through setup for the (very few) supercharged GT-350s, they did so for many good reasons. The most important of these had to do with simplicity – an irresistible option for a veteran racer like Mr. Shelby, and most of the guys in Inglewood at the time.

When you add more air with a super-charger, you need to add more fuel to match. With a fuel-injected engine, that usually means higher-flowing injectors, shown here on the right. You can't just add the injectors and go, you need to re-tune the system.

Putting the carb in a box and pressurizing the box with the blower is pretty basic compared to the other strategy, which involved putting the carburetor on the inlet side of the blower (draw through). This second approach is far more complex mechanically and from a tuning standpoint. There's a plumbing challenge, for one thing. From the outlet side of the blower, you need to move the atomized mixture through the rest of the intake tract – without the fuel dropping off onto the walls of the ductwork along the way. If that isn't handled properly, the engine runs lean until one of those puddles happens to blob its way near an intake port. Then the engine will run rich for an instant, and then resume its lean-running condition.

When you enclose the carburetor in the pressurized box, it just presumes it's running normally, except for the fact that the barometric pressure inside the box is a tad high. Since the entire carb is inside the box, all the air bleeds in the carb work normally. As long as the fuel pressure is regulated to maintain a reasonable margin to keep up with the pressure in the box, the fuel metering for boost conditions should be pretty close as well.

Tuning problems with a draw-through system usually involve fuel separation, which isn't usually a problem with a blow-through system. However, there is one fuel-system problem common to both setups: the sharp change in

fuel required when the system transitions between boost and no boost.

The transition from vacuum to boost happens quickly with any of the 'charger types discussed in this book. The change is so fast, in fact, that many fuel systems can't react quickly enough to prevent a momentary lean condition. Over the years, there have been a lot of talented people studying this phenomenon and working toward resolving it without resorting to the most obvious solution, which is to simply throw fuel at the engine even when it isn't running under boost.

Many of us are old enough to remember when computers were a bad thing (actually, this was just a nasty rumor circulated by the carburetor companies, and we all knew better). But we had no concept of how fast modern EFI systems would react to changing conditions. In a modern closed-loop system, the slowest part of the entire setup is the time it takes for red-hot exhaust gas to travel from the exhaust port to the oxygen sensor, and to have the sensor report to the engine's computer. At high RPM, that takes about 30 to 50 milliseconds.

Everything else in the system (meaning the timing and instructions to the fuel system) is being accomplished at much shorter intervals. In fact, that's why people are still working on the transition problem, because it's difficult to make the hydraulic aspects of a fuel system react as quickly as the electronic circuitry.

Throughout this book, there are many details on specific fuel-system

upgrades. While most aim for a similar effect, they are specific to a supercharger type and vehicle installation, so the details should be looked at relative to the particular project.

Ignition Upgrades

There's a special challenge created when the working pressure in the combustion chambers is bumped up significantly – the stuff in there gets harder to light.

Although you'd think that squeezing the mixture harder would make it easier to buzz an arc across a spark-plug gap, the reverse is true. The reason for this has to do with electron travel from tip to core across the plug gap. The familiar bluish arc that occurs in a plug gap is only the visible part of what is really happening there – trillions of electrons are migrating from one surface to the other, more or less, all at once. There are plenty more electrons where those came from, but the ignition system's job is to move about the same quantity of electrons each time, regardless of the effort it takes to move them.

That's the key to this situation – no matter how difficult it is to make the spark, the ignition system sends the same approximate number of electrons per cycle; only the length of time changes.

Here's an extreme example: Consider what would happen if you placed a sliver of wood into the plug gap. In order to make the plug fire, you'd first need to overcome the insulating qualities of wood. Compare that to when there's

One way to re-tune the engine after a supercharger installation is with an aftermarket chip. A chip can revise your fuel and spark curves to compensate for the extra air provided by the supercharger.

absolutely nothing between the core and tip of the plug. In both situations, there were the same amounts of electrons waiting to make the trip. As long as the tip and core are still attached, the electrons will be there, because they are literally contained in the atoms of the metal parts. While the wood prevented their travel across the gap, in the vacuum, they made the trip much quicker than usual. A spark plug will fire just fine in outer space – in fact, it will fire much easier than when installed in any engine. The process has nothing to do with air, except for the convenience and fun of viewing it with the human eye. Without air to ionize along the way, the migration isn't visible, but it still occurs.

In a supercharged engine, the mixture's molecules are more densely arranged than in a naturally aspirated engine, which makes it more difficult for the electrons to travel across the plug gap. Since there's more matter (air in this case) between the tip and core of the plug, the ignition system must do everything it can just to fire the plug. When that happens, the fast-moving electrons will whack a few of the carbon and oxygen molecules together, and combustion will begin.

Various ignition systems have different capacities. Some are able to move more electrons in one cycle than others. Modern cars have very powerful ignition systems because the manufacturers understand that a strong spark and a complete burn are necessary to keep emissions down. Even with a supercharger, you probably won't need much in the way of ignition upgrades, except for the correct plugs and wires, but the supercharger manufacturer's recommendations should be followed in any case.

Older ignition systems might require substantial upgrades to deliver a clean, reliable spark. Earlier ignition systems are often, but not always, inadequate for use with blowers, and must be upgraded to more contemporary electronics. Follow your supercharger manufacturer's recommendations if there's any doubt.

Spark-plug heat range is another consideration. Essentially, a plug's range refers to how quickly it can dissipate

An air-to-air intercooler puts the hot, compressed intake charge into indirect contact with the relatively cool ambient air (just like a radiator does with your hot coolant). The cooler air pulls some of the heat out of the warmer intake charge, cooling it down for better combustion.

heat into the surrounding cylinder head material. A plug with a short nose has a shorter heat path between the tip and the surrounding shell, so it's considered a colder plug. A plug with an extended nose will tend to run hotter because the path is longer between its tip and the threaded shell area.

Plugs don't have an easy life. Under normal circumstances, they aren't allowed to settle on a nice, stable operating temperature. Instead, they are subjected to sharp increases in temperature whenever you open the throttle. Even when the vehicle is cruising at a steady speed, the plugs see small variations in temperature. When selecting a proper heat range, you want a plug that stays hot enough to keep itself clean, but has the heat transfer capability to shed heat quickly when you stick your foot into the throttle.

Choosing the right plug is often a trial-and-error process, because your driving style and the terrain in the area will both contribute heavily to the decision. Generally, when you add a supercharger, you'll need a plug at least one heat range colder than stock. With the blower, your plugs will have to deal with higher combustion temperatures.

What's happened is that the engine is making more power, so there's more heat in the engine, and everywhere else under the hood.

Charge Cooling

Any effort to compress air will introduce heat, and that works against us when we want to keep the intake charge nice and dense. When air is warmed, it becomes less dense because the molecules are more active, so they move apart in giving each other a little "comfort space." When that happens, there are fewer molecules packed into a given space (less dense), making them less available for burning fuel. So, hot air works against your supercharger.

What we need here is something to keep a lid on the rising temperature of the air as it passes through the blower. We need a charge cooler. Some people call them intercoolers, some call them aftercoolers, but the idea is the same – to reduce the temperature of the intake air by pulling out some of the heat. For our purposes, let's agree to call them intercoolers.

An intercooler is very similar to a radiator. There are two types; one works exactly like a radiator – but in reverse –

With an air-to-water intercooler, a supply of cool water is circulated through a heat exchanger to remove some of the heat from the hot, compressed intake charge. An air-to-water intercooler can be quite effective, as long as the water stays cold.

using a cooler liquid to pull heat from the hotter air. This is called an air-to-liquid or air-to-water intercooler. The other type of intercooler uses relatively cool ambient air passing over the fins and core of the intercooler to pull the heat out of the warmer air inside. This is called an air-to-air intercooler. In either case, the heat comes out – coolness is not added in.

A heat exchanger (a more general term that engineers use for an intercooler) works by bringing hot stuff into such close proximity to cooler stuff that the heat is happy to jump toward it. In a typical radiator, the heat in the coolant is contained in a thin-walled, finned core that has a large amount of relatively cool ambient air flowing through it. The speed of the heat transfer is greatly affected by the density (actually, the specific gravity) of the media being heated or cooled. A radiator for the cooling system requires a very large airflow to be effective, because the temperature of the water is much slower to change than the temperature of air – that's why cars have fans to keep the airflow up when the car isn't moving. If there were an endless supply of ice-cold water flowing around and through the core, a fan would be completely unnecessary, because the heat in the coolant would happily and

immediately jump ship, leaving the coolant free to go back through the engine again.

With an intercooler, we know there will be hot air inside the gadget. It's the speed of the actual heat transfer that makes one of the two intercooler designs preferable. Heat will be sucked out of the hot intake charge much more quickly if there is liquid flowing across the outside of the core, provided that the liquid is cooler than the air inside. Using that speed premise alone, an air-to-liquid heat exchanger can have a smaller exchange (surface) area than the other air-to-air type.

Regardless of the cooler type, what's important is the temperature differential. The greater the difference in temperature between the air inside and the liquid (or air) outside will determine the efficiency of the intercooler to a large degree.

After a period of time, an air-to-liquid intercooler will heat the water or coolant until it's just as hot as the intake air charge, unless some provision is made to control the temperature of the liquid. When the two temps are equal, the intercooler is nothing but a bottleneck in the intake tract.

An air-to-air intercooler keeps working as long as there's adequate air-

flow around and through the core's fins. There is very little chance of the inside and outside temperatures equalizing unless the vehicle is involved in an equatorial African rally, and those cars use air-to-liquid coolers.

Given those distinctions, the big difference between the two types of intercoolers is the space required for the intercoolers themselves and their requisite plumbing. As stated above, the air-to-liquid intercooler is more compact, but it requires quite a bit of plumbing. An air-to-air type is larger and must be located where it has a good supply of air flowing through it. That real estate is sometimes hard to find, especially in Mustangs.

Exhaust Airflow and Temperature

With a supercharger, the engine will be burning more fuel and air. The exhaust system will probably need to be improved accordingly so it doesn't become a bottleneck in the system.

The exhaust gases will not only be more voluminous, they'll also be a bit hotter with a supercharged engine. This is the result of the larger amount of heat energy available from the increase in air/fuel being burnt. Engines create power by burning fuel inside the enclosed cylinders. The heat liberated from the fuel burnt in that process causes a pressure increase above the piston at Top Dead Center (TDC). Since there's nowhere for the heated gases to expand, the piston is pushed down the bore.

The particulars for various exhaust systems are included throughout this book. Be sure to check with the existing state-mandated laws regarding emission controls and the exhaust system.

Under-Hood Temperature Considerations

By now you understand that an engine making more power will also be generating more heat than stock. Not all of that heat is applied as rear-wheel horsepower, though. Much of it is lost through heat simply radiating from the engine. We've all opened the hood of a

With a crowded modern engine compartment, you need to be careful that nothing comes into contact with the really hot parts. There are many methods to keep under-hood temps down, including insulating the hot parts and moving more air through the engine compartment.

car that has been run hard, and then touched a radiator or header. Everything is hot under the hood, which should serve as an indication of just how much heat is not leaving through the exhaust pipe. The primary heat loss areas (after power production) in order are:

Exhaust gases
Cooling system
Radiated, under-hood losses
Convection (to the transmission)

With radiated losses ranking a solid third place, it's apparent why some attention should be paid to the items under the hood that can melt, especially those that are important for safety and reliable engine operation. Items of particular importance include the brake lines, for example.

Most supercharger installations would not require any rerouting of brake lines at all, but let's suppose one required you to alter the line coming from the master cylinder – a dangerous premise, agreed, but a good example of how to deal with a potentially bad situation. In our hypothetical scenario, we could create a barrier of some kind to protect the new brake line from as much engine heat as possible. The most effective heat barrier has always been distance, preferably

filled with free moving air. Next on the list would be a sheet metal barrier that allowed a good amount of relatively cool air to circulate past the line, while keeping the hotter, engine-side air away. This is very often completely feasible in an under-hood environment.

Barriers should be made of thin stainless-steel sheet. Aluminum is easier to work, but may actually form a heat

sink, drawing heat from the engine and actually warming the brake line (or other part) instead of protecting it. A thin sheet will also have a lower tendency to retain heat. Third, stainless won't rust and break the way a carbon steel barrier might if situated in a hot environment.

Most importantly, a barrier should be long enough and positioned so that it induces air movement between itself and the item you want to protect. Giving this aspect some concentrated thought will reward you in a part that might just be both pretty and effective.

When the car is moving, the general airflow under the hood enters through the radiator shroud/core support, passes across the sides of the engine, and exits under the firewall. When the car is moving more slowly, however, things get more complicated. Under-hood temperatures can literally triple if a car is caught in stop-and-go traffic. That's when you'll discover how effective your stainless barrier design will be.

Under those circumstances, fans are your only hope for air circulation, but there are some things you can use to your advantage there. When the fans are operating, airflow tends to move in a manner that is very useful to our purposes, just above what is called a boundary layer. Every surface under the hood has a relatively static layer of air between

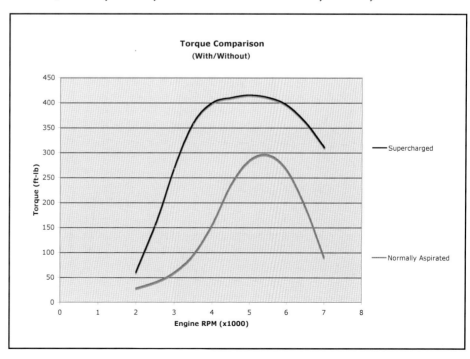

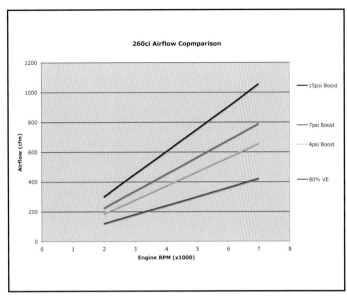

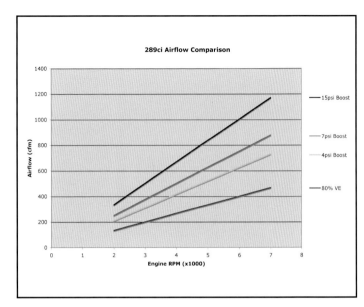

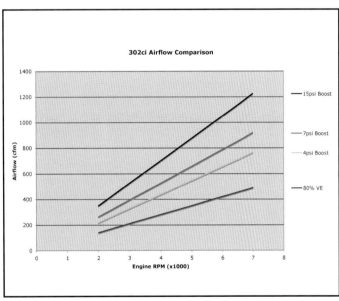

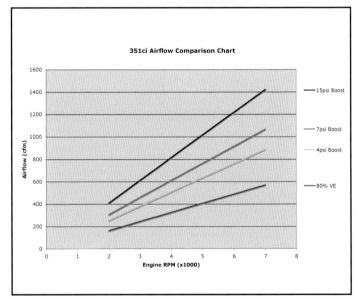

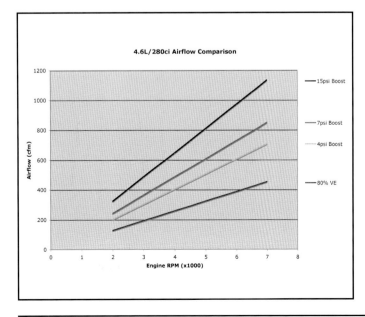

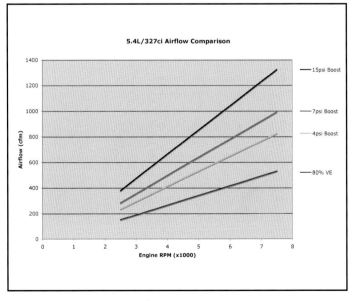

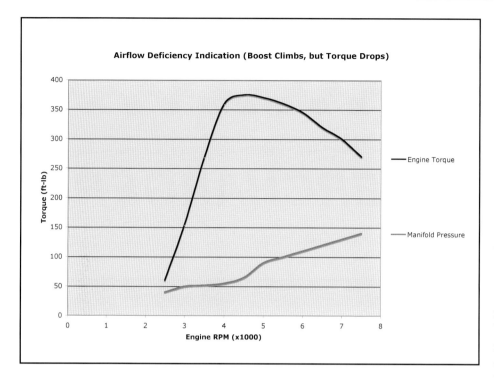

Airflow Deficiency Indication (Boost Climbs, but Torque Drops)

itself and any more animated air that may surround it. The useful aspect of this phenomenon is that as you close the distance to the boundary layer, the density of the air increases significantly from that of the circulating air. That means if we can somehow direct a bit of that dense air behind our barrier shroud it will be made much more effective. This wouldn't work as well as if we sent a torrent of cold air behind it, but it would help. As an example of this thinking, feed it air from the surface of the inner fender rather than from the firewall.

Cooling System Upgrades

The rule-of-thumb for cooling system upgrades is this: Proper maintenance is everything. That may sound like an oversimplification, but the truth is that today's cooling systems are designed with a considerable margin for error built in. They're engineered to stay functional even if they might become compromised by inadequate maintenance or from the natural effects of vehicle use and aging. This margin for error can compensate for the extra heat produced by your supercharger.

Keeping the cooling system healthy becomes much more critical when supercharging. Your best insurance is to follow Ford's recommendations precisely for the coolant specification and mixture percentages. If there are variations for regional weather situations, use the desert/high-temperature recommendations in every case. Those specifications typically suggest the best coolant mixture percentages for optimizing heat transfer through the radiator, which you'll need on a daily basis.

You should also shorten the periodic maintenance recommendations, possibly even cutting the intervals in half if you run it very hard on a regular basis. Coolant loses a certain amount of its effectiveness as it ages. This applies to its ability to aid heat transfer and fight corrosion and sediment in the cooling passages. Shorter service intervals will help keep the coolant behaving, as it should to prevent problems from the new heat load from the blower.

Although it might seem logical to use coolant without any dilution with water, in most cases, at least some mixture is recommended by Ford. A little water actually speeds the heat transfer ability of the coolant. Many gallon jugs of coolant on the market contain at least some water for this purpose. Make sure you don't leave any splashes of coolant on your garage floor or driveway after working on the system. This is especial-

ly true if you have a crawling baby or a family pet that might want to taste the stuff. It's extremely poisonous, even in small amounts, and can lead to death in some situations.

This plot shows a comparison between the torque theoretically available from a fresh and capable 302 with and without a supercharger. Torque is purely a function of cylinder pressure. The most important aspect here for the supercharged configuration is the area under the curve. As long as the supercharger can supply and maintain an elevated manifold pressure, the engine will make approximately the same torque over a very broad RPM range.

These plots show the calculated airflow for the various Ford small-block V-8s. In each chart, the lowest plot indicates the airflow for a naturally aspirated engine with an 80 percent volumetric efficiency (VE), which is what we get from a well-tuned high-performance street engine. The higher plots indicate the minimum airflow that should be used when considering upgrades to the intake tract when a supercharger is installed and set up to provide increased boost. Those numbers are based on a 100 percent VE. It is important to note that these plots do not account for faults in airflow through the engine from improper manifolding, poor camshaft choices, or the myriad of other snags that may exist in the total engine setup.

This plot shows what happens when there's a bottleneck in airflow through the engine. Notice how the boost pressure takes a turn upward at about the same point the torque starts to flag and drop off. The implication is that the blower is working fine, but at that point the engine cannot handle any additional airflow. The intake manifold starts filling up with air that never makes it into the cylinders. The airflow impediment might be anywhere from the intake ports to the exhaust pipe tips. Adding to the problem is the fact that the supercharger is forced to work very hard against the higher manifold pressure with no increase in power. It's a bad situation from every aspect.

ROOTS SUPERCHARGERS

It matters little whether you call them blowers, compressors, huffers, windmills, air transfer pumps, wheezers, Jimmys, or anything else. The supercharger in its various forms is almost as synonymous with high-performance enthusiasts as the beloved V-8 engine itself.

One of the more familiar superchargers is the Roots blower. It's considered by most to be the one that started it all. The Roots blower was first designed as a water pump, but it soon became clear that it was more effective as an air pump. People used it to solve a coal-mining problem, pumping fresh air in and methane gases out. One of the prerequisites for operating in such a dangerous environment was that the blower must not produce any friction or sparks. This turns out to be one of the reasons why we like the Roots blower so much.

In order to build something that will move plenty of air without any possibility of creating a spark, the design must be simple and hopefully not make any metal-to-metal contact as it does its job. The Roots blowers originally manufactured for ventilating mineshafts featured iron outer cases, but typically used wood rotors to actually move the air. When aluminum came into wide use, the non-ferrous metal was substituted for most of the components in the Roots, with the exception of the timing gears (manufactured from machined steel), which establish the relative positions of the two rotors within the case.

One of the major misconceptions about the Roots blower is that the air is moved straight down the center,

As a rule of thumb, any supercharger running a cog belt means business. If you want that classic look with that great blower whine, look no further than a Roots blower.

between the rotors. That's not true. In fact, the air is moved between the vanes of each rotor just inside the outer case of the supercharger. The rotors turn so that their vanes pass along the inside surface of the case in a downward motion.

The clearance between the rotor tips and the case must be small, but if it's too small, the tips of the rotors will rub against the case, especially at higher blower RPM. This isn't usually a problem on a properly setup Roots blower, but it will become extremely critical with certain other types of superchargers detailed later in this book.

There are other seals in a Roots blower that make a difference in its efficiency. In addition to the tip seals, there are annular or ringed seals located at either end of each rotor to seal them against the end plates of the blower housing. As you might expect, there are also oil seals on the rotor shafts to prevent the higher air pressure inside the supercharger case from moving oil away from the bearings.

There have been several rotor variations tried by the more innovative Roots supercharger builders through the years. The rotor configuration used in most of the early units, including all of the GMC types, involved a helical arrangement of the vanes and a tip shape (when viewed from the end of the rotor) that resembled that little paddle device your eye doctor has to hold in front of one eye as he tests the other. This vane shape allows one rotor to interact with the vanes of the other rotor, providing a fairly good seal against air leakage without the vanes actually touching. Without that unusual vane shape, the two helical rotors couldn't turn against each other without grinding to a screeching halt.

Drag racer Larry Bowers (Bowers Blowers) spent many years developing and refining one of the first practical straight-vane Roots-type superchargers. Although it seemed much simpler than the cast-aluminum helical rotors, there were several problems that required serious engineering time to make the straight-vane rotors work. Bowers, motives in pursuing this course included the much lighter net weight of a CNC-machine-cut billet rotor, higher compo-

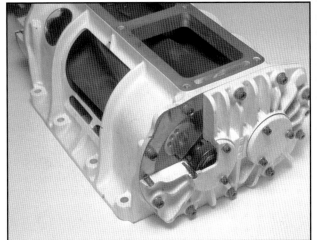

This cutaway of a Roots-type GMC 6-71 supercharger clearly shows the inner mechanical relationship of all the internal components. The supercharger snout, drive, and drive gears are at the front of the unit. These photos also show the rotors inside the case and the end plate. The Roots-type GMC supercharger prevents leaks by using a series of tip seals and annular seals at each end of the case. Oil seals on the ends of the rotor shafts prevent the higher pressure inside the housing from pressurizing the bearings. The rotors themselves are a helical design, although there have been several rotor variations tried on these blowers over the years.

nent strength, less rotor tip seal strength, and something we haven't discussed up to this point: adiabatic efficiency.

Adiabatic Efficiency

On the inlet side of an engine, heat buildup is the all-conquering enemy. Depending on what type of supercharger setup you select, the air flowing through the inlet system may be heated significantly when it's compressed.

Adiabatic efficiency is a number representing the amount of heat added by the supercharger system as a whole. In engineering terms, we're talking about the thermodynamic efficiency of the system.

A given supercharger will often come with a manufacturer's claim about its adiabatic efficiency, but the numbers for the whole system are a compound result of the individual components used between the air filter and the intake valve. In general, here is how the various power adders rank in terms of adiabatic efficiency, from lowest to highest (most efficient to least efficient):

- Roots helical-rotor blower
- Screw-type variants of the Roots design
- Centrifugal superchargers with external drive
- Turbochargers

The amount of boost employed, and whether or not the compression takes place within the supercharger, will have a great influence on how much heat is added to the inlet air charge. As a rule of thumb, the more compact the installation is, the less likely it will be to have a high adiabatic efficiency number.

With a traditional Roots blower, the amount of heat added by the supercharger itself is very low compared with most of the other supercharger designs (Roots screw or centrifugal scroll types). The reason for this is that a Roots blower isn't built to compress air as it operates – its effect is to feed the engine with (much) more air than would normally be contained within the intake manifold under normally aspirated conditions.

If you want to use a pump analogy here, the traditional Roots design is a simple transfer pump that isn't designed to raise pressure from its inlet to the outlet. Other supercharger types almost invariably are, indeed, built to elevate the inlet air pressure before the air intake charge leaves and goes on to the next part of the air inlet system. In engineering terms, a Roots is a pure blower, while almost all of the other supercharger types are actually compressors.

Screw-type variants of the Roots design actually compress air within their cases, and are usually followed in the inlet tract by an intercooler of some type. The intercooler counteracts the added heat from compression to keep the air dense.

Centrifugal superchargers also compress the air within their housings, but if the boost level is kept relatively low, they can still be used without an intercooler. For example, the Shelby GT-350 Mustangs that came equipped with the optional Paxton ball-drive, centrifugal supercharger had no intercoolers, and worked very well.

Turbochargers have gotten a lot more efficient recently because of highly sophisticated materials, but they still operate with the complication of bringing the inlet air within close proximity of the exhaust gases. The compressor side of a turbo raises the inlet air pressure and passes it along to the next component in the tract – usually an intercooler.

An intercooler is often required to maintain thermal-efficiency in a compressor, the payoff in measurable airflow at the intake valve almost always outweighs the added complexity in the system. As a total system, an intercooled compressor-type setup has a similar adiabatic efficiency to the Roots design, but with the advantage of higher net airflow.

Operational Levels

Up to a certain point, Roots-type blowers like the GMC and all aftermarket units patterned after it move air in a linear relationship to their rotor RPM or tip speed. For this reason, a Roots blower will tend to maintain a more constant boost level at the intake manifold than certain other supercharger types because the rotor RPM and crankshaft speed are directly linked via the drive belt.

The drive ratio of a Roots blower is critical for establishing a given intake manifold boost level. When a Roots blower turns at the same RPM as the crankshaft, it is said to have a 1:1 drive ratio. If the blower turns faster than the crankshaft, it is over-driven at a rate governed by the size of the blower pulley versus the size of the crank pulley. Conversely, if it is under-driven (again governed by the size of the blower pulley), it turns slower than the crankshaft. An example of an over-driven ratio would be if the blower turns at 1.2:1 times the crank speed.

This linear relationship does not hold true for superchargers that compress the air as it passes through (i.e., an Eaton), neither does it always hold true for Roots types once they're installed onto an intake manifold. The reasons for this are many, but the most obvious is that the engine will eventually form a restriction to the blower's output, regardless of its rotor RPM. At this point, additional rotor RPM will make no difference and the boost pressure will not continue to rise, because its maximum point is limited by leakage back through the supercharger, around and along its twisted rotors.

Hopefully, it will never matter to you, but an engine equipped with a Roots blower will continue to operate even if the blower stops turning. Of course, the causes for this are many, the least hazardous (to the equipment and your wallet) being the loss of a blower drive belt. In such a scenario, the engine won't run well, especially above a high idle, but it will continue to run, nonetheless. That's because of the air/fuel leakage taking place at one end of the intake

opening, along the rotor vanes, and down into the intake manifold at the opposite end of the rotor. This is particularly true of helical-type rotors.

Mini-Blowers

The Roots mini-blower has been around since the early 1950s with one of the prime examples being the Latham Supercharger, which experienced limited success in full-size 1953-'54 Lincolns. But it wasn't until the energy-conscious 1970s and 1980s that the small-displacement, high-RPM mini-blowers really came into their own.

The release of B&M Performance Products Street-Blower and Jerry Magnuson's Magna-Charger were both strong indicators that the blower boys were starting to think outside the traditional street-supercharging envelope. The Magna-Charger should not be confused with the Eaton high-speed, positive-flow, compact street supercharger(s) or the Eaton/Magnuson-produced high-speed, positive-flow high-performance street blowers that are currently enjoying huge acceptance with OEMs and the high-performance aftermarket. We'll discuss those later on.

When we speak of a "Roots mini-blower," we're basically talking about a compact version of the traditional Roots blow-through supercharger designed for use in tight engine compartments with a low hood line, as well as in vehicles equipped with a myriad of engine and emissions accessories.

Due to their very nature, these mini-blowers must spin at much higher RPM to achieve the same boost levels (up to 10 psi) as their larger-sized GMC-type counterparts. Of course, with higher RPM operating levels, these blowers require much tighter tolerances and higher-quality internal components.

Two examples of mini-blowers come to mind, although there have been a number of them over the years. One is the Holley/Weiand Pro-Street line and the other is the Blower Shop's Low Profile (Street) Supercharger, both of which will be covered in the Buyer's Guide segment of this chapter.

Unraveling Street Supercharger Mysteries

One of the most asked questions in regards to the Roots-type supercharger is, "what does it mean when you refer to a blower as being a 4.71, 6.71, 8.71, etc.?" To solve the mystery, we spoke with Craig Railsback, president of Blower Drive Service (BDS), one of the aftermarket's oldest and most respected blower manufacturers.

"The '71' connotation simply represents the cubic-inch displacement per cylinder for the motor designation originally used by Detroit Diesel. For example, if it were a GMC supercharged 2-cylinder inline diesel engine, the designation would be '2.71.' If it was a GMC supercharged 4-cylinder inline diesel engine, the designation would be '4.71,' and if it was a GMC supercharged 6-cylinder inline diesel engine, the designation would be '6.71' to represent the number of cylinders the engine had!" Railsback continued.

"In later years, Detroit Diesel also came along with the V-Series blowers (V-6.71 and V-8.71) to go along with their V-6 and V-8 diesel-powered engines, as well as debuting their V-92 Series for use with their lager displacement diesel engines. Today, the nomenclature '71' is used strictly to describe the type of blower, or size in question. It doesn't have anything to do with the actual size, or type, of engine you're actually installing it on."

While we had Craig's ear, we also asked him another question that many people often ask. "How big is too big?"

"It's usually sized according to the application. For example, one of our customers runs a 14.71 BDS supercharger on a Jim Oddy-built, stroked 420-ci Ford 351W engine that runs on straight alcohol. Obviously, that is a special application, which requires a larger-size supercharger. Typically, for a street car, you're looking at a small-bore 6.71 street supercharger because a stock-stroke 289/302-ci Ford engine really doesn't need that much supercharger."

What about compression ratios? How much (compression) is too much?

"Ideally, on street applications (due to poor fuel quality, etc.), it's a pretty

High RPM, small-displacement superchargers made a comeback in the late 1970s and early '80s. Shown here is a B&M Performance Products street blower, mounted on Herb McManken's highly modified early-model Mustang convertible. Note that this application uses a pair of Mikuni side-draft carburetors.

good idea to keep the boost and compression levels fairly low, and they (the engines) typically can't hurt themselves. For example, on either a 289/302-ci Ford pushrod V-8 or Ford 351-ci pushrod V-8 engine, 8.5:1 compression and 8.5 lbs of boost is an ideal pump gas combination."

And with this combination what would be an ideal (blower) drive ratio?

"If it's a 302-cid engine, it would be advisable to run about 5 to 10 percent underdrive to make about 7 to 8 lbs boost. With a 351-ci engine, it would be advisable to run a 1:1 drive ratio to make about 5 to 7 lbs of boost. Remember, the compression ratio and the octane fuel you use generally limit the amount of boost allowable, because detonation is always a serious factor."

How much carburetion is too much carburetion?

"The ability of an engine to consume air is in direct relationship with the cubic-inch displacement of the engine, the engine RPM, or operating level, and the amount of boost that you're intend-

ing to run. We have a formula (which is published in the BDS catalog) by which you can actually calculate that out and determine what size, and the amount of carburetion, you'll want to run on a particular engine."

What about electronic fuel injection?

"The ability to 'size' a system is a by-product of the air control device being used and the ability to provide the correct size of fuel line and fuel injectors to actually feed the thing. Quite typically, we use the same formula that is used on a carbureted engine to size the system accordingly."

The State of the Street Supercharging Industry

We've already established the fact that the traditional full-size Roots, or GMC supercharger, is *the* street and competition supercharger of choice with high-performance enthusiasts because of its looks, performance, and availability. With virtually millions of these blowers

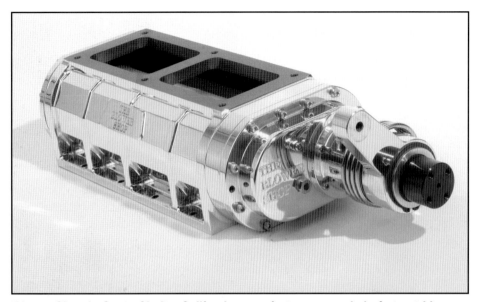

Blower Shop in Santa Clarita, California, manufactures a myriad of street blowers, competition blowers, and blower applications – including a Ford 429-460 big-block blower kit. However, its new CNC-machined, billet-aluminum 192 and 250 small-displacement, high RPM superchargers (max boost 10 psi) are the closest thing they have to adapt to a Ford small-block. The company is currently working on a kit.

out there on the market (manufactured by GM's Detroit Diesel Division until 1992), you could say a rather healthy street blower industry exists.

While many of the smaller blower shops still base their business on rebuilt GM cores, the industry itself is moving away from blower remanufacturing and concentrating on producing a better product by building their own cases, rotors, gears, end plates, and blower drives. In fact, these days it's entirely possible to buy a complete "GMC" street supercharger using all new components.

"For a longest time, the standard has been to rebuild these old superchargers replacing whatever parts needed to be replaced along the way," says Kevin Peters, president of Kuhl Superchargers. "Then, as useable supercharger cores started becoming harder and harder to find, the industry started manufacturing all new external pieces, (cases, end plates, etc.), but still used the core rotors and gears out of old Jimmy blowers. In recent years, however, the core quality of these parts has gone down dramatically. After Roger Penske purchased Detroit Diesel from GM approximately 12 years ago, he converted the product line over to turbochargers. So there have been no

new Diesels produced with blowers on them for over 12 years. And that means no more service replacement parts. Now we manufacture our own rotors and gears, etc.; everything is brand new, front-to-rear!"

Not surprisingly, manufacturers like Kuhl, BDS, and others also supply these smaller blower shops with product(s), so what you're actually talking about here is an industry within an industry. Now let's take a closer look at the supercharger manufacturer's (listed in alphabetical order,) who service, support, and motivate the Roots blower industry.

The Blower Shop

Beginning with the acquisition of Bowers Blowers in 1984, the Blower Shop primarily served the Top Fuel, Funny Car, and Top Alcohol dragster classes and drag boat market. The Santa Clarita, California-based company was instrumental in the development of leading edge Roots-blower technology. They manufacture examples of the famed supercharger in 6.71, 8.71, 10.71, 12.71, and 14.71 sizes.

The Blower Shop will build you a big-block (429-460) Ford street supercharger kit on request. More importantly, the company has new 192-cid and

250-cid low-profile street blowers. Blower Shop superchargers are CNC-manufactured from 6061, T-6-aluminum bar stock. The supercharger cases measures 8⅝ inches from the top of the blower to the carburetor base plate (billet carburetor adaptor sold separately), which makes them ideal for any small-block-powered early- or late-model Ford cars, trucks, and even street rods.

The input shaft and coupler are heat-treated 4340 steel. Its drive gears are also heat treated and specially ground for longevity and smooth operation. This unit uses a 16-rib drive belt, and a total of seven different top pulleys (available in either V-belt or serpentine) are available to provide up to 10-psi boost.

The Blower Shop only offers their 192-cid and 250-cid mini-blowers for small-block Fords.

The Blower Shop
26846 Oak Avenue, Units C&D
Santa Clarita, CA 91351
Phone: (661) 299-5483
Fax: (661) 299-5485
www.theblowershop.com

Blower Drive Service (BDS)

Established in 1969 in a one-car garage in Whittier, California, BDS has gone on to become *the* top manufacturer in the high-performance Roots-blower aftermarket. However, unlike many of your blower manufacturers who started out building race blowers, and then developed a line of street blowers, BDS started out as (and continues to be) a street blower specialty company, although they do build some impressive competition blower setups as well.

In regard to the street blower segment of the market, BDS is dual faceted. The company will service, rebuild, and update versions of the popular GMC supercharger. They also offer over-the-counter Jimmy's using BDS-developed components. BDS was one of the first in the industry to manufacture replacement parts and upgrade components for these blowers, and today, they are clearly the largest.

BDS also manufactures their own blower cases (in everything from 4.71

BDS is a multi-faceted company. They can either rebuild an original GMC-type core blower for the customer using all-new BDS-manufactured parts, or they can sell you one of their own setups based on everything from a BDS 4-71 to 16-71 supercharger housing.

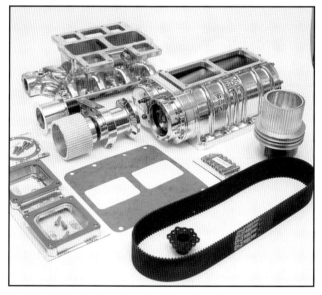

BDS offers a total of three street blower kits for the Ford 351W V-8 engine. Variance depends on the amount of accessories (smog pump, alternator, air conditioning, power steering, etc.) the engine is equipped with.

to 16.71 sizes), along with their own intake manifolds, blower pulleys, blower drives, carburetor plates, fuel-injection plates, fuel-injection throttle bodies, air scoops, blower cams, engine management systems – you name it!

"Probably one of our real claims to fame is the fact that if it came equipped with a popular American V-8 engine, we probably offer an intake manifold and a kit to fit that particular engine," laughs Craig Railsback, and he's not kidding!

All told, BDS offers street blower kits for a total of seven different automotive manufacturers, with a total of 106 applications! When it comes to Ford products, BDS manufactures 26 different setups ranging from the 289/302 up to the 429-460 Ford big-blocks – Boss 429 included.

Starting with the 289/302 pushrod V-8, BDS offers a total of three street blower kits based on the actual engine accessory packages (power steering, alternator, air conditioning, smog pump,

etc.) you plan on using. They are:

p/n 526-3S1/2: BDS 289/302 3-inch 1v 6.71
p/n 526-3S2/2: BDS 289/302 3-inch 2v 6.71
p/n 526-3S3/2: BDS 289/302 3-inch 3v 6.71
p/n 566-3S1/2: BDS 351W 3-inch 1v 6.71
p/n 566-3S2/2: BDS 351W 3-inch 2v 6.71
p/n 566-3S3/3: BDS 351W 3-inch 3v 6.71

* In recent years, the popularity of the Ford 351-Cleveland ("C") engine has been decreasing, due much to the fact that parts for these engines are becoming scarce, and with the implementation of EFI into Ford's product

BDS also manufactures blower rotors, including its exclusive Air Lok competition blower rotors.

BDS also offers three street blower kits for the 289-302W-based Ford small-block V-8 engine. They also manufacture kits for the Ford Boss 302, the Ford 351 Cleveland, and the Ford 400M small-blocks.

To accommodate a number of popular brand carburetors (shown here are Holleys), BDS manufactures its own carburetor intake plates in either cross-mount or tandem applications.

With both street and competition blowers being built nonstop, the back shop at BDS is always a beehive of activity.

line in 1984 (and the subsequent conversion of the 351 Windsor to EFI), the 351 Cleveland has sort of taken a back seat. Nonetheless, BDS still stocks a total of three kits for this engine, and another three for its second cousin, the slightly larger Ford 400M, which uses a larger supercharger. They are:

p/n 536-3S1/2: BDS Ford 351-C 3-inch 1v 6.71

p/n 566-3S2/2: BDS Ford 351-C 3-inch 2v 6.71

p/n 566-3S3/2: BDS Ford 351-C 3-inch 3v 6.71

p/n 578-3S1/2: BDS Ford 400M 3-inch 1v 8.71

p/n 578-3S2/2: BDS Ford 400M 3-inch 2v 8.71

p/n 578-3S3/2: BDS Ford 400M 3-inch 3v 8.71

Blower Drive Service (BDS)
12140 E. Washington Blvd.
Whittier, CA 90606
Phone: (562) 603-4302
Fax: (562) 696-7091
www.blowerdriveservice.com

Holley-Weiand

Holley Performance Parts recently acquired both the B&M Street Supercharger product line and the Weiand Equipment Company (say, "why-and"). This gave the carburetor king a staggering lineup of street-strip blower hardware, ranging from the ex-B&M Street (mini) Blower to the complete Weiand line of GMC Roots-type street blower kits.

Surprisingly though, the manufacturing giant only offers a total of three applications for the Ford small-block V-8 engines from the vintage Ford 21-stud Flathead V-8 (hey, that's a small-block) to 289/302 W-style engines. The proverbial centerpiece for these kits is Holley/Weiand's low profile, 177 Pro Street long-nose supercharger. Holley/Weiand claims (horse) power gains of 25 to 40 percent are entirely realistic. In each application, this blower comes with its own dedicated intake manifold, along with a 10-rib blower drive, lower crank pulley, and all the necessary support systems accessory brackets.

p/n 6551-1 (satin), 6552-1, (polished): 177 Ford
    Flathead Pro-Street Kit

p/n 77-174FSBS-1 (satin), p/n 77-174FSBP-1
    (polished): Holley/Weiand 177 Ford Small-
    Block Pro-Street Kit

The big news at Holley these days is the manufacturer's 50-state legal Holley

Holley/Weiand's entry into the Ford small-block street blower wars is somewhat limited. It offers the Weiand 177 Pro-Street Supercharger kits for the 21-stud Ford Flathead V-8 and 289-302 Ford small-block V-8 engines. These blowers are touted to deliver between 25 and 40 percent more power (10 psi) and feature Teflon-tipped rotors for longer blower life.

Holley offers a 50-state-legal Holley Thunder street blower system for the 1997-2004 5.4L 2-valve mod motor Ford F-150, Ford Expedition, and Lincoln Navigator models. This intercooled blower is capable of producing 390 hp and 445 ft-lbs of torque at the flywheel. Could a 4.6L SOHC and DOHC Mustang mod motor application be forthcoming? Time will tell!

1966 MUSTANG PRO STREET COUPE

"This was my very first car," says commercial electrician Russ Fielding. "I purchased the coupe from my mother, Donna, back in 1975 when I was just 17 years old."

Of course, this Porsche India Red and yellow-flamed '66 Mustang has seen numerous incarnations in the 29 years that Fielding has owned it. But let's cut to the chase and talk about its current life.

"My sons Chris, Cory, and Casey and I welded the chassis together right here at home in our garage," says Russ. "I sent the exact specifications for the chassis to Chris Alston at Alston Chassis Works, and he bent everything up, and shipped it back. Then we welded

everything together right here at home."

With the chassis completed, Fielding and his sons started bolting on suspension parts. Up front, the Mustang features Flaming River rack-and-pinion steering, along with a Chassis Works Avenger IFS bolted up to a set of Wilwood Engineering four-piston calipers and Heidt's Hot Rod Shop 2-inch-dropped front spindles. Also along for the ride are Air Ride Technologies (ART) air bags and Toxic front shocks.

Out back, the Fielding family's '66 utilizes a Fab-9 narrowed Ford rear end equipped with a set of 11-inch Wilwood Engineering six-piston disc brakes and 4.56:1 Strange gears. It's all suspended by a Chassis Works four-link setup with

Air Ride Technologies air bags and Toxic coil-over shocks, and a set of Chris Alston's finest wheelie bars.

The wheels and tires on the coupe consist of 15 x 4.5-inch E.T. 16-spoke (front) and 15 x 15-inch Weld Racing (rear) wheels wrapped in Mickey Thompson Pro Street rubber.

DSS Racing machined and assembled the 1983 Ford 351W engine. Starting from the bottom up, the engine features a Probe Industries 408-ci stroker kit with a set of Eagle 4340 forged-steel H-beam connecting rods, an Iskenderian blower cam, and a set of 8.5:1 DSS forged-aluminum pistons with Seal Power rings. Up top you'll find a pair of TFS Twisted Wedge aluminum

UP IN FLAMES

cylinder heads sporting ARP and Isk-enderian valvetrain hardware, protected by a pair of Moroso sheetmetal valve covers. Bolted in-between is a BDS 10.71 supercharger operating at 8 psi, and a pair of 750-cfm Barry Grant Demon carbs. The '66 features an MSD ignition system and a somewhat exotic thermal-coated 3-inch exhaust system from the talented crew at Doug's Head-ers. Backing up all of this supercharged power is a C-4 transmission with 3,500-rpm B&M stall converter. The final link in the '66's power train is an Inland Empire custom-fabricated driveshaft.

The Fielding's '66 was painted by Mike Todorovitch in PPG Porsche India Red with yellow- and -blue pin-striped flames by California Designs. It makes a real statement in both performance and looks. This Mustang is also some-what luxurious with its Mark Lopez-stitched Kat Skin tan leather and tan wool carpeted interior and trunk area. Yes, this is one awesome supercharged pro-street Mustang!

Thunder Power-Charger Kit for the 1997-2004 5.4L-equipped, 2-valve Ford Expedition, Lincoln Navigator, and Ford F-150s. This kit is reputed to boost the power of your 5.4L SOHC mod motor to an incredible 390 hp and 445 ft-lbs of torque.

This kit comes with the Holley Thunder 144 Power-Charger supercharger, a dedicated intake manifold, 10-rib supercharger drive belt and tensioner, and fully integrated liquid-to-air intercooler with Earl's AN fittings. The air and fuel are handled by a Power Shot conical air filter kit, an 80-mm CNC-machined 6061 billet-aluminum throttle body, Holley boost compensator regulator, and a 225-lph electric in-tank fuel pump. A Holley Thunder Power Chip, all the brackets and fittings, complete instructions, and Holley Thunder fender logos are also included. Holley also hints of a 4.6L SOHC and DOHC Holley Thunder package for the Mustang GT and SVT Mustang Cobra models in the near future.

p/n 300-520: Holley-Thunder 144 Power-Charger
    5.4L Kit

Holley-Weiand
1801 Russellville Road
P.O. Box 10360
Bowling Green, KY 42102-7360
Phone: (800) HOLLEY
Tech Line: (270) 781-9471
www.holley.com
www.weiand.com

Kuhl Superchargers

Mike Kuhl, famed Top Fuel engine builder and car owner, established Kuhl Superchargers (just say "Kool") (Kuhl & Olsen "Revell Fast Guys" AA/FD) back in 1970. Initially, the company only built blowers for use in drag boat racing and professional drag racing. Kuhl branched out into the street blower aftermarket in the early 1980s with his big-block Chevrolet street blower kit, which became a big success.

In December 2001, Mike Kuhl sold his company to longtime employee/engineer Kevin Peters. Peters expanded the Kuhl product line to 12 kits, with over 25 different fitments and/or applications.

For Kuhl's small-block Ford street

Kuhl Superchargers of Santa Ana, California, offers street blower kits for both the Ford 289-302W and the 351W small-block V-8 engines. Kuhl manufactures every component under one roof – blower cases, intake manifolds, blower drives and gears, carburetor and throttle body intakes, and fuel systems.

supercharger program, the Santa Ana, California-based supercharger manufacturer has taken a rather (dare we say it) "Kool" approach, with a decidedly high-tech twist.

"We offer two street supercharger kits for the 5.0L (302 ci) and 5.8L (351W) Ford small-block V-8 engines," says Peters. "Rather than milling off the top of a conventional 4-barrel intake

manifold and welding on a plate, what we're doing here is using the 5.0L and 5.8L Ford truck rectangular EFI intake manifold base, and bolting an adaptor plate up to it! The welded two-piece carbureted (4v) intake manifold has been the standard in the industry ever since the first street blower kit was designed for this application. First of all, with this type of approach, rarely if ever do you

Above left: Of course, the centerpiece for every Kuhl street supercharger kit is one of its Kuhl Kased superchargers, available in 4-71 to 14-71 configurations. Above right: Kuhl Superchargers offers blower intake manifolds based on either a 302W or 351W square-port EFI intake. These manifolds maintain the correct runner length and bolt to the top plate, rather than having to be welded. But the real benefit is that you have the option of plugging up the ports and running carbureted or injected, using all factory Ford EFI hardware. This setup also works with an Edelbrock, Holley, or TFS aftermarket square-port EFI lower intake manifold.

Another advantage of the Ford small-block Kuhl Supercharger system is the cog belt pulley that drives the water pump, which considerably simplifies things. Kuhl's small-block Ford setups also use the damper to reduce crank belt vibration, lengthening the service life of the crank snout and the balancer.

get the intake runner length right due to the fact that you're machining off an integral part of the manifold, so you're sacrificing low-end torque and some degree of horsepower right off the bat. Secondly, with the use of a plate welded to the top of a modified 4-barrel intake, you often run the risk of warp-age problems due to it being welded.

"We've chosen the Ford truck base because it's readily available. It features an excellent runner length and intake port volume, and due to the fact that you already have the fuel injector bungs plumbed into the base, you can either plug them up and run conventional carburetors (with carburetor plates available for Holley, Barry Grant Demon, or Edelbrock 4v carburetors) or set it up to run with electronic fuel injectors and twin 70- or 75-mm throttle bodies. Either application will also work with an Edelbrock, Weiand, or Trick Flow Specialties (TFS) EFI lower intake manifold, as they are all basically the same as the Ford. You can even use the stock Ford ignition and stock Ford fuel rails and fuel regulator with this setup. It's a really neat system!"

1951 FORD CLUB COUPE

Body man Steve Whitlock's wild, '51 Ford Club Coupe, a.k.a. Pro 51, never fails to wow them the minute Steve rolls it out of the trailer. "It's a real jaw dropper," says Whitlock, of his mildly massaged '51 Ford with '50 Ford front-end sheetmetal. Of course, a lot of that has to do with the Troy Williams-applied Dupont candy purple topcoat with vermilion ghost flames.

The minute you look inside, you can't help but wax nostalgic about the Red Jones-stitched purple-and-white tuck-and-roll interior, complete with a pair of late-model Mustang GT bucket seats, a Grant GT wood rim steering wheel, and Paul Hatchett custom dash with SVO instrumentation.

The '51 features a Jim Norman-modified chassis with a Fat Man Fabrications Mustang II IFS, Flaming River rack-and-pinion steering, disc brakes, and Carrera coil-over front shocks. Out back there's a Carrera-suspended, narrowed 9-inch Ford rear end with its humongous Mickey Thompson-equipped Cragar-Weld aluminum modular wheels.

The one single item that gets our attention the most is that awesome BDS 6.71-supercharged 341-ci 1970 Ford 351W engine with its twin 600-cfm Holley double pumpers sticking through the hood.

Machined and assembled by Clegg Machine Works in Provo, Utah, Whitlock's blown Henry features mechanical appointments like a set of Trick Flow Specialties (TFS) Twisted Wedge aluminum cylinder heads, a set of Speed Pro 8:1 compression forged-aluminum pistons, a Crane cam and valvetrain, Melling oiling system, Pete Jackson gear drive, Mallory ignition, and Sparker Per-

THE PURPLE FLURP

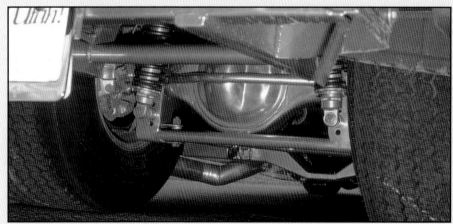

formance four-tube headers with War-lock mufflers. An owner-assembled 1970 Ford C-6 backs up the healthy powerplant.

Whitlock drives his supercharged '51 regularly, and the coupe has won numerous awards, including a mention at the Good Guys Pleasanton, California, show. Steve is currently putting the finishing touches on his 11th car, a purple pro street 1957 Ford Ranch Wagon. But it's going to have to be awful, awful nice to beat Steve's Pro 51!

Rather than manufacturing a complete line of blower kits, blower manufacturer Mert Littlefield of Littlefield Blowers, Anaheim, California, prefers concentrating on building top-quality street and strip superchargers (in 6-71 to 14-71 sizes) and related components. Littlefield finds it more cost-effective to assemble kits from readily available components within the aftermarket rather than stocking a huge inventory of items.

Of course, the actual centerpiece with either setup is one of the company's fully polished "Kuhl Kased" 6.71 superchargers.

"This blower is brand new from the ground up. It features one of our fully

polished 6.71 Kuhl Kases, along with brand-new billet-aluminum end frames, a new front cover equipped with brand new gears, and rotors. It's an all-new supercharger!

"Another interesting feature about our Ford kits is that we drive the water pump with a cog belt pulley, and we use the factor Ford damper rather than a crank hub so that the life of the crank will be increased (less vibration)."

Listed below are the part numbers for Kuhl Superchargers Kits:

p/n 02401-62: 5.0L/289/302 Street Supercharger Kit
p/n 02404-61: 5.8L/351W Street Supercharger Kit
p/n 02402-63: 351-C Cleveland Street Supercharger Kit

Kuhl Superchargers
2222 West Second Street
Santa Ana, CA 92703
Phone: (714) 547-7071
Fax: (714) 547-4170
www.kuhlsuperchargers.com

Mert Littlefield Blowers

Longtime Funny Car racer Mert Littlefield originally worked for Danekas Superchargers, but purchased the company in 1974. Annual sales of approximately 250 new Littlefield street and strip 6.71 to 14.71 superchargers a year, plus a thriving rebuild business, keep Mert and his staff of 10 very busy!

Customers include street machiners, nostalgia racers, tractor-pull racers, mud bog racers, and monster truck racers. Unlike the bigger guys, Littlefield likes to focus on one sale at a time. In regard to prepackaged small-block Ford street supercharger kits, Littlefield doesn't offer one.

"We build our own superchargers and our own blower drives. However, we don't offer a Ford small-block kit per se. What we usually do is purchase the intake manifold, and anything else the customer specifies, from a company like BDS, and then ship them their 'kit.'"

Littlefield Blowers
1114 East Kimberly
Anaheim, California 92801
Phone: (714) 992-9292
Fax: (714) 992-1717
www.littlefieldblowers.com

Mooneyham Blowers

Famed drag racer Gene Mooneyham has been building street and strip superchargers since 1951. The company offers a full line of both aluminum and magnesium blower cases in everything from 6.71 to 14.71 configurations, along with a complete line of support hardware.

Like Littlefield, Mooneyham manufactures his own superchargers but doesn't offer a small-block Ford street blower kit. You'll have to build one yourself!

Mooneyham Blowers
1935 West 11th Street, Unit N
Upland, CA 91786
Phone: (909) 985-4425
Fax: (909) 985-4435

Littlefield Blowers specializes in rebuilding Roots/GMC cores along with selling and servicing its own product line, which keeps a staff of 10 plenty busy year-round.

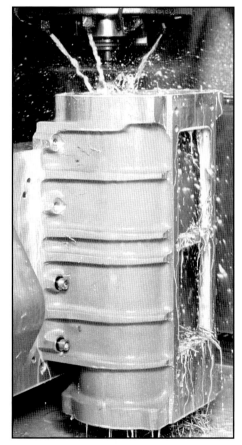

Mert prefers to do all his work in-house, and that includes machining his own aluminum and mag blower cases. This magnesium-cased 16-71 competition supercharger is being machined.

Gene Mooneyham offers some street blower kits, but he prefers to keep things simple by focusing on the manufacturing of his own blowers for the most part. Mooneyham Blowers is also a dealer for Cragar, SCS, Gearbox, and RCD Engineering Products.

1965 Pro E.T. Mustang Coupe

This isn't your ordinary street/race Mustang coupe you're looking at here, folks! This car was pro-built for one thing and for one thing only: tearing up the drag strip!

Powering Charlie Hamilton's blue-and-white-striped beauty is a Jim Oddy-assembled (Oddy Perfection) 420-ci alcohol-burning 351W. The engine is assisted by an Enderle-injected, front-discharge, high-helix 14.71 BDS supercharger bolted to a Hogan sheetmetal intake, the very same combination that's used on the IHRA Pro Mod cars. It makes 1,500 hp and 1,300 ft-lbs of torque.

The foundation for this potent setup starts with an SVO 351W cast-iron block outfitted with a Scat stroker crank, a set of Kryptonite alloy connecting rods, JE pistons, and an Iskenderian cam. Bolted up top is a set of Dart aluminum cylinder heads with an Iskenderian valvetrain. The ignition system is an MSD 7AL unit fired by a Blaster coil. A set of BMR 2¼-to-4-inch stepped headers and 4 x 18-inch Dynomax mufflers handle exhaust duties. Backing all this awesome power is a Triple-J Transmissions Powerglide with a 5,600-rpm Hughes Performance stall torque converter and a trans brake.

Of course, all the power in the world isn't going to go anywhere unless you have a reliable chassis to bolt it up to. Whittier, California's Advanced Design Fabrications (ADF) built the Mustang's Super Gas framework using an Alston Chassis Works front and rear frame assembly joined together by a common 12-point roll cage.

Up front, the Mustang utilizes an Alston/Koni strut front suspension, a Ford Pinto manual rack-and-pinion steering box, and a set of Wilwood Engineering front disc brakes. Out back, Charlie's Mustang utilizes Alston four-link/Koni coil-over suspension bolted up to a standard Ford 9-inch rear axle (narrowed 4 inches) equipped with an M-W Enter-

prises third member, 4.10:1-geared spool, and 40-spline axles. Rear braking comes from of a set of Strange Engineering rear disc brakes. Wheels and tires consist of a set of Weld Rod-Lite 15 x 3.5-inch and 15 x 15-inch wheels and Mickey Thompson E.T. Street and Firestone racing rubber.

In keeping with the pure-race theme, Hamilton's Mustang uses a one-piece lift-off Al Fiberglass Mustang front end. Paint and bodywork was done by Greg of West Covina in PPG Viper Blue with Wimbledon White racing stripes.

On the inside, Hamilton's '65 has a pair of JAZ fiberglass bucket seats, Simpson Safety Equipment, ADF interior panels, a Painless Performance switch panel, Auto Meter liquid-filled instrumentation, Fuel Safe fire safety system, a trunk-mounted 16-gallon JAZ fuel cell, and dual Sears Die Hard batteries.

Hamilton and his rapid Mustang are regulars at both Irwindale Speedway's eighth-mile track, where the car has recorded a best of 4.90 at 150 mph, and Palmdale, California's L.A. County Raceway (LACR) with a best of 7.70 at 172 mph in the quarter. Man, now that's hauling!

CENTRIFUGAL SUPERCHARGERS

Any self-respecting Ford enthusiast will be somewhat familiar with centrifugal superchargers. The premise is simple, even if the execution is not. Air molecules have enough mass and weight so that if you build a device to propel them from point A to point B quickly enough, they'll tend to keep moving in that direction. If you trap these molecules inside an intake manifold, static pressure will build. Centrifugal superchargers use an impeller to do the propelling.

If you think about the term "centrifugal" in terms of a supercharger, you might think it must take one hell of a spin to thrust air into an engine with anything more than atmospheric pressure. The impellers used on either turbochargers or centrifugal superchargers require high tip speeds to compress air. Tip speed is relative to the diameter of the impeller, requiring higher RPM for smaller diameters, or a lower RPM for a larger diameter, to attain a given tip speed.

There are two practical ways to spin an impeller at such high speeds:

1. With a turbine, as used in a turbocharger and described elsewhere in this book.

2. Mechanically, using power from the engine's crankshaft and a method of compounding it from a few-thousand RPM to tens-of-thousands RPM at the impeller. This is how it's done in a centrifugal supercharger.

Small-block Mustangs and Shelby's were available with a Paxton centrifugal supercharger in the later 1960s. The entire carburetor was simply enclosed in a box.

An impeller should be a masterpiece, incorporating the results of many sciences. To work well, this core part of a centrifugal supercharger must be designed around a detailed understanding of airflow dynamics, material properties, and careful machining techniques. If any of those areas are overlooked, the supercharger in question will not provide the anticipated performance, or it may just fail entirely.

Impeller design is very important because of its extremely high operational speed – up to 60,000 rpm in some applications. Another factor is efficiency; the shape and contour of the blades and voids determine its ability to accelerate air within a specific range of rotating speeds. In this particular aspect, the shape of the housing that surrounds the impeller, referred to as the volute, is critically important for the impeller to achieve its intended efficiency.

The basic centrifugal supercharger design has been used to supercharge engines almost since the appearance of the four-stroke engine itself. Innovators like Indy 500 great Harry Miller took impeller design to its practical limits in automotive and marine racing engines as early as the 1930s. For Miller's famed and fabled 750-hp Novi V-8 (originally commissioned by a Novi, Michigan, Ford dealer), the 10-inch impeller enlisted turned at a speed that caused the outer tips of the impeller blades to travel at Mach 1.6.

Impossible? Well, because the impeller was moving so much air, the density around those supersonic tips was high enough to prevent the shock waves that destroy most metal parts moving at that high a speed.

At the point where air is delivered from the impeller circumference to a diffuser, its mass has been accelerated and its volume reduced. In other words, the air has been (greatly) compressed. In a reverse of the venturi principle, a diffuser provides an increasing cross-sectional area for the air, slowing it down and increasing its static pressure. The compressed air will only move back through the impeller if the tip speed drops significantly or if the static

Robert Paxton McCulloch's 1953 release of his new VS-57 found favor on cars such as the short-lived 1954 Kaiser Manhattan, the 1956 Studebaker Grand Hawk, the 1957 Packard Clipper, and 1958 Packard Hawk.

pressure on the intake tract exceeds the pressure change across the impeller.

The relationship between impeller speed and how efficiently it will accelerate an incoming air mass is governed largely by:

1. The shape of the impeller blades and the cavities among them.

2. The shape of the impeller housing and the diffuser cavities.

3. Clearances between the impeller housing and the impeller's blades.

4. The positioning of the impeller and the housing surface behind it.

Every impeller design has a speed range where it's highly efficient at moving air. With today's computer-aided design (CAD) and automated profile machining, these RPM ranges tend to be fairly wide, but that wasn't always the case. Incredible as it may seem, Harry Miller was forced to experiment with a lengthy series of one-off impellers, each one an investment casting requiring many hours of finishing and balance work, before he discovered one with the right contours to suit the available drive speed of the Novi racing engine.

Within the sweet spot of an impeller's efficiency range, the dynamic sealing between the blades and housing improves to the point where the system begins to seriously tax the inlet airflow characteristics and whatever might follow the supercharger in the sequence of intake components. This means that when the blower starts to get in its performance curve, anything in the rest of the intake tract that can't handle the flow will seriously compromise the net effect of the supercharger. While this is true regardless of the general type of supercharger installed on an engine, it is particularly true with the centrifugal types because of the remarkable change in airflow that can take place with a very small change in engine speed.

This effect is similar to – but not nearly as dramatic as – the radical shift in performance that occurs when the impeller of a turbocharger enters its sweet spot. During these transitional

Shown in this cutaway of the McCulloch VS-57 is: The variable ratio blower pulley, the manifold pressure-activated solenoid air valve used to control air-piston movement, the compressed coil spring pack, air supply passageway, supercharger air outlet, impeller shaft pilot bushing, planetary drive balls, the units impeller shaft which is 4.4 times the pulley speed, labyrinth oil seal, small diameter magnesium impeller, the air inlet, the units series of five ball driver cups that rotate the five drive balls within the fixed outer race, the pulley shaft ball driver, the split outer race bearing which pre-loads the drive balls, the units 14 coiled springs which set the pre-load split on the outer bearing race, the unit's piston type oil pump, and the VS-57's lubricating oil reservoir.

Shown here are examples of the NASCAR version and street version of the McCulloch VR-57 ball-drive centrifugal supercharger. The blower on the left is the Daytona NASCAR version, which was briefly used by the Ford teams (1957) prior to its being outlawed. The unit on the right is the street version (with 3.5:1 to 5.5:1 step-up ratio) that was successfully used on the 1957 Ford Blower Bird, of which a total of 211 cars were built.

periods, the airflow through the entire intake tract changes drastically, which is why something as simple as a loose air filter element or an intermittent leak in ducting can wreak havoc with the engine's air-fuel metering, especially with EFI or SEFI systems.

During the mid-1950s, Robert Paxton McCulloch first sold small centrifugal superchargers that could be installed on automotive engines without too much difficulty. Paxton's reciprocating-ball drive blowers were homologated for use in NASCAR by Ford Motor Company, who offered a similar application for their 312-ci engines and made them available in the two-seat, '57 Ford Thunderbird and a limited number of full-size Ford models.

These early units differed in one specific sense, according to Craig Conley of Paradise Paxton, a division of Paradise Wheels Inc. "Although both units incorporated a ball-type drive mechanism, the NASCAR units had what amounted to a direct drive for the impeller, while the street versions used oil pressure to exert variable tension on the outer races of the drive, allowing engine speed to somewhat regulate how effectively the impeller was driven. Higher oil pressure brought about a change in drive ratio in the ball drive, and the impeller speed went up accordingly. It was the ball drive that eventually became the obstacle for those seeking higher boost pressures. The ball-drive units are perfect for anyone looking to generate 7 lbs of boost or less – they'll do that quietly and reliably. Above that manifold pressure, the impeller should be driven by a more direct method, such as the modern gear drive units."

Using a gear system, like the one used in Paxton Novi superchargers, to drive the impeller is one way to eliminate slippage and impeller speed loss within the supercharger itself. While both designs (reciprocating-ball and gear drive) are actually belt driven from the crankshaft (so there's one over/under-drive ratio there), the extreme overdrive ratio required to attain the proper impeller speed happens within the supercharger housing itself.

The precise origin of the gear-driven centrifugal supercharger remains a hotly contested point. Of course, Harry Miller's Novi supercharger was turned by a beautifully crafted gear drive that linked one of the camshafts to the impeller.

Robert Paxton McCulloch also built a gear-driven centrifugal supercharger around 1937, which pre-dates his reciprocating ball design (originally developed in 1943 as an air pump for the U.S. Navy) by almost half a decade. However, Paxton's crankcase lubricated, gear-driven model for the Ford Flathead V8-60 was noisy and deemed impracticable from a mass-production standpoint.

Others also tried it with limited success, and it wouldn't be until the early 1990s when Vortech Engineering LLC popularized the gear-driven centrifugal supercharger, changing the face of the street supercharger industry.

The Paxton Reciprocating-Ball Drive

In the past, Paxton superchargers used a unique ball drive to overdrive the impeller relative to the size input pulley and shaft speed. The impeller turned approximately 4.4 times faster than the input shaft speed. The drive arrangement is nearly silent, which is a significant difference from the gear-drive units. It's a relatively simple drive system, but its operation is often confusing to grasp.

Paxton's ball drive was an important feature of the units built by the company to circulate air inside America's submarines during World War II and later in nuclear submarines. In that application, even very small mechanical noises are telegraphed through the hull of a ship into the surrounding water, immediately revealing the boat's position to a potential enemy.

The input shaft on a silent-drive Paxton supercharger drives a precision-cast separator with drive lugs positioned between the balls. The balls are contained in a stationary two-piece outer race. The race is split along the circumference, and the two sections are spring-loaded together with considerable force.

Here's an example of a Paxton SN-60 supercharger. It is the same unit that Andy "they call me Mr. 500" Granatelli used at Bonneville to set numerous land speed records while driving a 1958 Studebaker Hawk. Granatelli was so impressed with the Paxton SN-60 that he and his brothers bought the company.

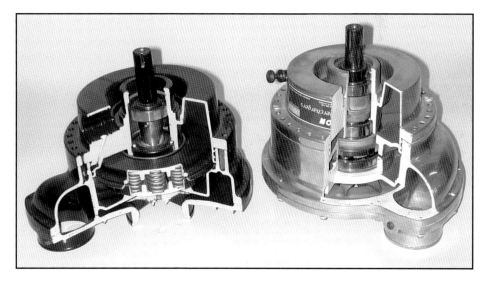

This photo shows cutaway models of both the Paxton SN-60 (left) and SN-2000 (right). Forty years of engineering, refinement, and improvements are quite obvious.

The spring loading between the two sections of the outer race creates pressure between the ball surfaces and the impeller shaft to spin the impeller efficiently without using drive gears.

To accomplish this, the impeller shaft features a concave section to accommodate the balls, which exert considerable pressure against the shaft, thanks to the spring-loaded outer ball race. Because the balls capture the impeller shaft, it rotates at their surface speed – resulting in an impeller speed that is about 4.4 times the speed of the supercharger's input pulley.

The actual overdrive ratio is calculated by comparing the circumference of the outer race (at the point where the balls contact it) with the circumference of the concave section of the impeller shaft. From a math-geek's standpoint, however, the ratio is much more complicated, because the balls, outer race, and impeller shaft do not present a system with clearly defined contact points. The balls contact the impeller shaft (and the outer race) across an arc, or segment, of their outer surface, rather than a single point on any of the diameters.

Adding to the confusion, this contact area is somewhat affected by the RPM of the system. At very high rotational speeds, the balls get "heavier" against the surface of the spring load

Internal heat buildup has always been a problem with Paxton's SN Series reciprocating ball-drive superchargers. Paxton's answer was the dipstick oil cooler, designed to recirculate the fluids through a small heat-exchanger radiator. The unit was reportedly capable of dropping oil temperatures by 150 degrees F.

The OE automotive project, which really vaulted the Paxton name into the limelight, was the Paxton-supercharged 1966 Shelby GT 350 Mustang. Rated at 306 hp from Shelby American Inc., a Holley-carbureted Paxton SN-60 street blower setup would boost the horsepower rating of the Hi-Po 289 K-motored Ford small-block up to 375 hp – registering a 68-hp gain! This factory-installed option could be ordered through Shelby American Inc. on the 1966 through 1968 model small-block cars, as well as from Ford dealers with applications from 1965 to 1970 small-block Ford V-8s.

between the two outer race sections. This has the effect of further altering the contact areas and reducing the overdrive ratio by a very small amount.

Paxton Products: The Early Years

The product name "McCulloch" pre-dates the "Paxton" trade name by some three years. After perfecting his reciprocating-ball design air pump, which served the U.S. Navy so well (and more sophisticated versions of the original design still do), Robert Paxton McCulloch took $700,000 in research money and set up shop in Los Angeles, California. His first product was the McCulloch VS-57 supercharger, released in 1953.

Close to 46,000 McCulloch VS-57s were produced, and the unit achieved notoriety, as well as some degree of success, on cars like the 1954 Kaiser Manhattan, the 1956 Studebaker Golden Hawk, the 1957 Packard Clipper, and the 1958 Packard Hawk.

In 1956, McCulloch set up a special automotive service parts division known as Paxton Products. That same year, the company released a new variable-rate supercharger known as the VR-57, which featured a step ratio from 3.5:1 to 5.5:1, achieved by a spring pack that would change the distance between the ball races based on engine RPM. This is the same supercharger that was briefly used in NASCAR competition, as well as being used on some 211 '57 Ford "Blower Birds."

In 1958, Andy Granatelli set numerous land speed records at the Bonneville Salt Flats driving a Paxton SN-60-equipped Studebaker Hawk. That same year, Andy, Vince, and Joe Granatelli purchased Paxton Products. The Granatellis wanted to service and maintain the manufacturer's government contracts with the military, to maintain the company's lucrative automotive replacement parts business, and perhaps sell a little new product here and there.

In 1965, Paxton was again vaulted into the automotive limelight when Carroll Shelby teamed up with them first on a blown '65 289 Shelby Mustang and later on a twin-blown 427 Cobra, which Carroll personally sold to comedian Bill

Cosby, but it was never made a production item. The Paxton supercharger option was produced in limited quantities on Shelby GT-350 Mustangs from 1966 to 1968. This setup was also available as an over-the-counter, dealer-installed option on standard small-block V-8 Mustangs from 1965 to 1972.

In the gloomy 1970s, Paxton focused on other markets, yet continued to sell the SN-60 and related service components. Then, in 1979, Ford came out with the Fox platform Mustang. Paxton immediately responded with their compact, SN-60-based kit designed for the carbureted 5.0L.

Ford changed all that in 1986 with the newly re-engineered 5.0L Mustang LX and GT models, which featured Sequential Electronic Fuel Injection (SEFI). Paxton Products was the first aftermarket supercharger manufacturer to release a 50-state-legal street supercharger kit using an updated version of their SN-60 reciprocating-ball-drive supercharger known as the SN-89. In essence, the EFI Mustang and the Paxton SN-89 (later updated to SN-92, SN-93, SN-95, and SN-2000 versions) basically rewrote the book on emissions-legal street supercharging.

Were it not for the introduction of the 5.0L (302ci) engine Fox Platform Mustang in 1979, Paxton Products may have languished indefinitely. In 1985, the Santa Monica, California, blower house released its SN-60-based street supercharger kit for the Mustang V-8 models. It was basically a redesign of the old carbureted Shelby GT 350 kit. With the 1986 introduction of the 5.0L engine Sequential Electronic Fuel Injection (SEFI) Mustangs, Paxton literally blew the lid off the market with the release of its 50-state-legal street supercharger kit. Paxton refined this application over the years with the release of the SN-92, SN-93, and SN-2000 5.0L-based street supercharger packages. Shown is the final SN-2000 incarnation installed on Craig Conley's first-generation 1993 SVT Mustang Cobra.

The New Kids on the Block

At this point, let's introduce a handful of "new players" into the fold. In 1992, Paxton engineers Jim Middlebrook and Jim Wheeler left Paxton Automotive Products and founded Vortech Engineering. Vortech Engineering became the first manufacturer in the street blower business to introduce a helical cut, gear-driven, crankcase oil-lubricated centrifugal supercharger to the mass market with the release of their emissions-legal Vortech V-1A. Middlebrook and Wheeler realized the shortcomings of the Paxton ball-drive design, while recognizing a VERY healthy market, and had done their homework on the significant challenges in manufacturing a saleable product.

Vortech realized that the largest of these obstacles was building a gear drive that could operate at very high speed and remain reasonably quiet. The answer came from an existing technology, as is often the case when performance enthusiasts adapt this or that looking for more horsepower.

Vortech found what it was looking for in a gear-cutting firm that made parts for helicopter gearboxes. Although fairly simple in appearance, gears are extremely sophisticated in terms of their tooth profiles, balance, and surface finishes, especially when intended for high-speed applications. In order to build the gear drivetrain Vortech had in mind, the teeth of the larger input gear and smaller impeller gear required very precise machine work to keep them from sounding like a police siren.

With the release of the V-1A, Vortech became the first to bring a gear-driven centrifugal supercharger to the mass market. Vortech simultaneously released their 5.0L late-model Mustang and their 7.5L (460-ci) Ford F-150/F-250 truck street blower kits. They have never looked back.

The structure of the new company changed approximately one year later after a falling-out between Wheeler and Middlebrook. In his departure, Jim Wheeler started up his own company, Wheeler Racing-Powerdyne Automotive Products, Inc., producers of the Powerdyne BD-10 (and later BD-11) silent-drive centrifugal street superchargers. These Powerdyne blowers sort of resemble a Paxton or Vortech in appearance, but are internally totally different in design.

Internally, the Powerdyne BD-10 differs from the Vortech V-1A in that it uses an internal cog drive belt (much quieter) rather than high-pitch helical-cut drive gears. It also uses ceramic ball bearings and is 100 percent self-lubricating.

In order to keep critical start-up money and cash flow on the positive

WHAT'S BIG, RED, AND GOES REAL FAST?

Pro 5.0L classes almost look like "cookie cutter" classes with one late-model Mustang after another out there competing. However, there are still a few individuals out there who march to the beat of a different drum. For instance, Howard Cody is a bona fide, distant relative of "Buffalo Bill" Cody himself! Cody is very into everything from the Outlaw and Street Outlaw classes to the Modified Street and True Street classes.

Rather than building a state-of-the-art late-model Mustang, Howard plans on making his mark in the NMRA Street Outlaw class driving this ultra-radical '71 Mustang Grande. Cody's 'Stang gets its kick from an intercooled D3-R ATI ProCharger setup. The engine consists of a 9:1 compression RDI tall-deck aluminum 351W block equipped with Robert Yates/Cox Racing-prepared high-port aluminum heads, a Moldex crank, Carrillo connecting rods, Ross pistons, and a Competition Cams

camshaft and valvetrain. That's backed up with a Lenco 5-speed planetary transmission with a 3.32:1 first gear and a RAM Automotive clutch.

"This is essentially the same setup that they run in the late-model Pro 5.0L cars," said Cody. "However, this type of setup has never been tried in a car like this before!"

A closer inspection of Howard's wild ride reveals a rather unique induction system based on an Edelbrock Victor Jr. 5.0L EFI intake, highly modified by cylinder head specialist Ron Cox. First, the manifold was cut in half and angle-milled 0.0915 inch to fit the Windsor wider intake valley and Yates cylinder heads. Then Cox drilled the intake runners to accept a set of Bosch 160 gal/hr fuel injectors, which are controlled via a F.A.S.T. engine management system. Once that was all done, the manifold was welded back together.

To add to the plumbing nightmare, Cody's '71 Mustang Grande also features a forward mounted Spearco 4-gallon intercooler fed by an off-site reservoir that can hold up to 8 gallons of chilled coolant.

"Fabricating the front motor plate and installing the Lenco transmission also proved challenging. After all, this is an old racecar, and everything had to be either modified, or we started over from scratch, and that included building the fiberglass hood, which my wife, Jo Ann, and I did at home in our garage!

"My friends tell me that I should take the drivetrain out of this heap and transplant it in a late-model Mustang. But I don't have any desire to do that. Right now, this car is a one-of-a-kind. I mean, nobody at the racetrack is going to have himself or herself a Street Outlaw class '71 Mustang Grande like this. Were I to do whatever everyone else says I should do, I would be just another face in the crowd."

THE FLYING BRICK!

The creation of Powerdyne Automotive Products based in Lancaster, California, resulted after estranged partner Jim Wheeler split with Vortech Engineering approximately one year after the founding of the company. The by-product of that split was the 50-state-legal Powerdyne Automotive Products-manufactured silent drive BD-10 – a 100 percent self-lubricating street supercharger. The BD-10 initially found its way into the engine compartment of the Fox Platform Mustang and was extremely successful. The Powerdyne BD-10 and BD-11 successors were also private labeled to B&M Automotive Performance Products, and SVO/Ford Motorsport, a.k.a. Ford Racing Technologies (FRT).

1986 to 1993 5.0L Mustangs. In essence, the ATI ProCharger featured the best of both worlds. The unit was self-lubricating like the Powerdyne BD-10, but it also possessed the reliability and strength of precision-ground steel-drive gears like the Vortech V-1A trim.

Is it Paxton, or is it Paxtons?

Initially that query may be pretty confusing, but like everything else in life, there is a point. In 1998, investor David Adams Jr. purchased all the corporate assets and production rights to the Paxton Supercharger from the Granatelli family. Adams was a businessman first and a car enthusiast second, and his primary intent was to regain the company's rightful market share, which it had been steadily losing to the likes of Vortech, Powerdyne, and other new manufacturers.

In order to do that, Adams realized that Paxton had to create an all-new product that could go head-to-head with the top-selling Vortech V-Series product line. The Novi gear-driven supercharger, so named after the Granatelli-owned Novi Indianapolis 500 racecars, was already on the drawing boards. Adams was also keenly aware that it was going to take a sizeable amount of capital to finance such a project, and took stock of the company's assets. Since the original Paxton ball-drive SN-60 design had seen its day, he brokered the sale of the product line to well-known Shelby restorer and vintage Paxton and McCulloch supercharger tuner/rebuilder Craig Conley of Paradise Wheels Inc. Conley received the remaining inventory, all engineering rights, and the entire original tooling from those earlier units.

"Actually, there really wasn't anybody taking over the rebuilding of the McCulloch and Paxton superchargers," said Conley. "Since I had a passion for the vintage Shelby Mustangs, I started rebuilding these units on my own back in the early 1980s without actually being an authorized Paxton dealer.

"Once Paxton got wind of the fact that I was rebuilding these units on my own, and had a real good success rate

side, Powerdyne private labeled its new silent running BD-10 to B&M Performance Products with the release of its BD-10-based street blower model.

Powerdyne also attracted the attention of Ford Special Vehicle Engineering (SVO) a.k.a. Ford Motorsport, largely due to the fact that the BD-10 was 100 percent self-contained. This appealed to Ford because a customer could install

one of these 50-state-exempt street blowers on any 1986 to 1995 5.0L-equipped Mustang or any 1996 to 2001 5.0L Ford Explorer or Mercury Mountaineer SUV without negating any manufacturer's warranties.

Another new arrival was Accessible Technologies, Inc. (ATI) with their 50-state-legal ATI ProCharger self-contained, gear-driven supercharger for the with these blowers, a gentleman who worked for Paxton named Brian Berry contacted me and asked me if I would be interested in coming up and doing sort of a 'cross training' program with their engineers. Paxton had been having some reliability problems recently with their SN-Series blowers, and thought that perhaps I might be able to help out."

That initial introduction opened the door for Conley. Before too long, Craig began working on some joint engineering projects with the manufacturer, and in fact, the factory was actually sending some of their warranty repairs directly to him.

"Paxton was kind of winding down their SN-Series reciprocating-ball-drive blower program and getting into their Novi gear-drive blower program because that's what everybody wanted. I was asked if I would be interested in taking over the McCulloch and SN-Series parts, sales, and repair business from the years 1953 to 2000. In a nutshell, I was just at the right place at the right time!"

However, as good as the Paxton Novi 1000 and 2000 gear-drive blowers were, and are, the monumental expense of bringing these products to market proved a bit too much for the company. In late 2001, Paxton Automotive Products and Vortech Engineering LLC entered into what was officially called a "strategic partnership," where the two product lines were consolidated under the Vortech Engineering LLC corporate umbrella.

THE STATE OF THE CENTRIFUGAL SUPERCHARGER INDUSTRY

Accessible Technologies, Inc. (ATI)

ATI's ProCharger took the 5.0L pushrod V-8 ranks by storm in 1994 with the release of the P600 gear charger, which produced up to 17 psi! The company next released the P600B, making it the first gear charger over 5- to 8-psi to be awarded a 50-state-legal exemption.

ATI next came out with the D-1 race blower in 1998, which holds the distinction of powering the first "Pro 5.0L" Mustang into the 7s (7.60 at 185 mph).

The updated production version of that blower is the ProCharger D3R. The company's latest offering is its P-1SC, which is a fully contained, self-lubricating gear-drive supercharger capable of producing 800+ horsepower!

Perhaps one of the ATI ProCharger's strongest selling points (aside from offering incredible amounts of boost) is the fact that the company offers either air-to-air or air-to-water intercooler packages with the large majority of its

ATI ProCharger's P-1SC is the company's bread and butter product. It is 50-state-emissions-legal and widely used on a variety of popular street and strip applications up to 925 hp.

ATI ProCharger offers a 4.6L 3-valve system for the 2005 Mustang GT models.

5.0L and 4.6L supercharger kits. ATI ProCharger also offers two kits for the popular 3.8-liter Mustangs. ATI ProCharger has introduced a new street supercharger kit for the 3-valve 4.6L 2005 Mustang GTs. Carbureted Ford small-block owners will be happy to learn that ATI ProCharger also manufactures a kit for the 289/302 and 351W small-block engines.

1999-2001 V-6 Mustang, p/n 1F1212-SCI, 9-psi w/P-1SC

1994-1998 V-6 Mustang, p/n 1DJ212-121, 9-psi w/P-1SC

1986-1993 V-8 Mustang, p/n 1FAO11-SC, 6-20-psi, w/P-1SC

1986-1993 V-8 Mustang, p/n 1FA212-141, 9-14-psi w/600B or P-1SC

1986-1993 V-8 Mustang, p/n 1FA214-SCI, 14-20-psi w/P-1SC

1986-1993 V-8 Mustang, p/n 1FA324-D1, 17-25-psi, w/D-1 or D-1SC

1994-1995 V-8 Mustang, p/n 1FBo11-SC, 6-15-psi w/P-1SC

1994-1995 V-8 Mustang, p/n 1FB212-141, 9-14-psi w/P600B or P-1SC

1994-1995 V-8 Mustang, p/n 1FB324-D1, 15-22-psi w/D-1 or D-1SC

1982-1985 V-8 Mustang, Same as '86-'93 5.0L

1999-2001 Mustang GT, p/n 1FE212-081, 8-psi w/P-1SC

1999-2001 Mustang GT, p/n 1FE212-121, 10-12-psi w/P-1SC

1996-1998 Mustang GT, p/n 1FD212-101, 8-10-psi w/P600B or P-1SC

1996-1998 Mustang GT, p/n 1FD212-121, 10-12-psi w/P-1SC

1996-2001 Mustang 2v/4v, p/n 1FX204-D1, Race Kit w/D-1SC

1996-1998 Mustang Cobra, p/n 1FC212-061, 6-psi w/P600B or P-1SC

1996-1998 Mustang Cobra, p/n 1FC212-101, 10-psi w/P600B or P-1SC

1999 Mustang Cobra, p/n 1FF212-061, 6-psi w/P-1SC

1999 Mustang Cobra, p/n 1FF212-101, 8-10-psi, w/P-1SC

Accessible Technologies, Inc. (ATI)
14801 West 114th Terrace
Lenexa, KS 66215
Phone: (913) 338-2886
Fax: (913) 338-2879
www.procharger.com

Powerdyne Automotive Products also worked in conjunction with FRT to engineer a BD-11-based street supercharger kit for the 1996-2001 5.0L engine Ford Explorer and Mercury Mountaineer SUVs. A total of three part numbers are available for these models. Shown in these photographs is the author's one-of-a-kind Saleen XP/8 Mercury Mountaineer SUV, which was one of the R&D mules used by the Lancaster, California, blower house for FRT reprototyping, testing, and final certification.

Ford Racing Technologies

FRT offers a total of seven street blower applications based on the Powerdyne BD-11 self-lubricating, self-contained centrifugal supercharger, available for both the 1986-1995 5.0L Mustang (except Cobra) as well as the 1996-2001 5.0L Ford Explorer and Mercury Mountaineer, and 1993-1995 5.8L SVT Lightning pickup. Some are 50-state-legal, while others are not. They are:

1986-1993 5.0L Mustang except SVT Cobra (6-psi), p/n M-6066-A50

1986-1993 5.0L Mustang except SVT Cobra (9-psi), p/n M6066-A51*

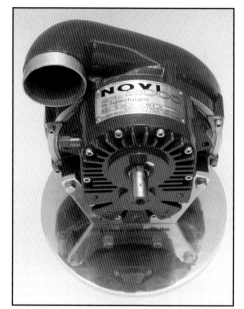

Internally, both the Novi 1000 and Novi 2000 models feature similarities like the same geartrain, internal bearings, and supercharger intake. The discharge tube, volute, and turbine wheel design are the same also. However, through the Novi 2000's unique impeller and compact scroll design, the unit is capable of 27-psi boost and can sustain it at 900+ hp ranges.

Paxton Automotive has redesigned its fabled 1964-1968 carbureted blow-through street supercharger kit for 260/289/302W small-block Ford engines and the 1969 351W Mustangs (available in either passenger-side or driver-side applications). This was done as a tribute to the limited-production Paxton supercharged Shelby GT 350 Mustangs. The company's new gear-driven Novi 1200 is used as the centerpiece.

1994-1995 5.0L Mustang except SVT Cobra (6-psi), p/n M-6066-B50

1996-1997 5.0L Explorer & Mountaineer (6-psi), p/n M-6066-E50*

1998 5.0L Explorer & Mountaineer (6-psi), p/n M-6066-E51

1999-2001 5.0L Explorer & Mountaineer (6-psi), p/n M-6066-E52

1993-1995 5.8L SVT Lightning (6-psi), p/n M-6066-T51

*Not legal for sale or use on pollution-controlled motor vehicles.

www.fordracingparts.com

Paxton Automotive Products

Although Paxton Automotive Products, Inc. is now owned by Vortech Engineering, LLC, it operates as a separate entity. In 1998, Paxton entered a new chapter in its storied history when it replaced the aging SN-60-based, reciprocating-ball drive supercharger with the Novi 1000 and Novi 2000 standard rotation and reverse-rotation gear-driven superchargers.

The Novi 1000 was designed to appeal to the sport-compact enthusiasts as well as V-8 enthusiasts. It's capable of producing a wide range of boost using various-sized pulleys, with a maximum boost rating of about 12 to 15 psi.

On the other hand, the Novi 2000 centrifugal supercharger was designed for up to 27 psi, while delivering up to 700 horsepower. The Novi 2000 RR was specifically designed for use on the 4.6-liter Mustang GTs and SVT Cobras, and is the largest, most powerful reverse-rotation centrifugal supercharger available. Both of these blowers are available in either satin or polished finish.

Paxton has also just released their Novi 1200 model to cover the medium-output street applications (7½ psi), such as vintage street machines like the Shelby GT-350.

Also available is the race-only Novi 3000, which is reported to feature a 40 percent larger volute than the Novi 2000 model, with a whopping 5-inch inlet diameter and a 3½-inch discharge tube.

This blower also featured a 3.54:1 step-up ratio, cryogenically treated internal moving parts for extra strength, a 201-alloy cast-aluminum impeller, and billet-steel helical-cut gears. Like the Novi 1000 and 2000 models, the 3000 is available in either standard drive or reverse rotation in either satin or polished finish.

1986-1993 Novi 2000 5.0L H.O. Mustang V-8, p/n 1001810

1994-1995 Novi 2000 5.0L H.O. Mustang/Cobra, p/n 1001812

1996-1997 Novi 2000-RR 4.6L SOHC Mustang GT, p/n 1001813

1999 4.6L Novi 2000-RR 4.6L SOHC Mustang GT, p/n 1001815

2000-2004 Novi 2000-RR 4.6L SOHC Mustang GT, p/n 1001822

1996-1998 Novi 2000-RR 4.6L DOHC SVT Cobra, p/n 1001814

1999-2004 Novi 2000-RR 4.6L DOHC SVT Cobra, p/n 1001816

2005 Novi 2000-RR 4.6L SOHC 3-valve Mustang GT, p/n 1001851 (satin), p/n 1001851-P (polished)

FAST ORANGE MOD-MOTOR MUSTANG

This Vortech T-Trim Mod Motor Mustang runs mid-9s with ease! Racer Lidio Iacobelli owns a very lucrative 5.0L and mod-motor Mustang tuner shop called Alternative Automotive Performance. Of course, a lot of fast Mustangs run out of Lidio's shop, but one of the fastest and quickest belongs to the boss himself.

Iacobelli runs this bright tangerine-colored 4.6L DOHC '98 Mustang Cobra to compete in the NMRA Mod Motor Mustang class. At this writing, Iacobelli and his Vortech T-Trim (26 psi) Cobra have run a best of 9.43 at 144.00 mph – and we hear that the car can run a lot quicker. Now let's take a closer look at this beautiful machine.

The Mustang's chassis was prepared by Mike Pustelny Race Cars (MPR) and employs a Pustelny Race Cars combination 2 x 3-inch rear subframe and 12-point roll cage that joins up with the existing Mustang sheetmetal sub structure in front. The rear consists of an MPR-narrowed 9-inch rear end with 5.43:1 Strange Engineering gears, suspended by a Koni coil-over four-link suspension. Rear braking comes in the form of a pair of Lamb Engineering disc brakes.

Up front, Pustelny also installed a lightweight tubular Koni front strut suspension with Lamb Engineering front disc brakes and Flaming River rack-and-pinion steering. The Mustang rides on 15 x 3.5-inch (front) and 15 x 15-inch (rear)

Center Convo-Aero modular-aluminum wheels. It rolls on 15 x 7-inch Pirelli tires up front, and a set of 15 x 32-inch Mickey Thompson E.T. drag slicks in the rear.

Powering this brute is an Alternative Automotive Performance-prepared 4.6L DOHC mod motor outfitted with a set of 9.8:1 compression Diamond Automotive forged-aluminum pistons, AAP-prepared DOHC crank and connecting rods, a set of AAP-prepared 4-valve DOHC cylinder heads featuring a 3-angle valve job, and AAP custom-grind cams and valvetrain. The intake side consists of a BBK throttle body and K&N conical filter. The exhaust flows through a set of thermal-coated Performance Fabrications Engineering (PFE) 1⅞-inch primary stepped headers with 3-inch collectors and a set of Flowmaster two-chamber mufflers. Backing up this potent combination is a Performance Automatic-prepared

GM 700R4 equipped with a Stallion torque converter.

On the inside you'll find the aforementioned 12-point MPR roll cage, along with a set of MPR aluminum bucket seats trimmed in orange and black vinyl upholstery by Port Huron's Willie's Workshop. Also on board is RJS safety equipment, AutoMeter instrumentation, and a B&M Pro-Comp shifter. And yes, since Lidio's Mustang competes in a "street car" class, that factory Mach 460 stereo is fully functional!

The lightweight Cobra R-Model hood on Lidio's Mustang comes from the folks at H.O. Fibertrends. Credit for the striking PPG Tangerine Orange paint goes to Joe Cicall. As NMRA Mod Motor Mustang drag cars go, this is one of the nicest!

Paxton's 50-state-legal 1989-1993 5.0L Mustang pushrod V-8 kit is available with either the Novi 1000, which pumps out 5 to 6 psi, or the Novi 2000 supercharger, which pumps out 8 to 10 psi.

Paxton's new reverse-rotation (RR) Novi 1200-based street blower kit for the all-new 4.6L 3-valve 2005 Mustang GTs received rave reviews when it debuted. This kit is reported to deliver up to 50 percent more horsepower operating at 8- to 9-psi non-cooled.

1964-1968 Novi 1200 carbureted
Mustang/Cougar/Comet/Falcon/Fairlane
260-302, passenger-side mount, p/n
1001839 (satin), p/n 1001839-P (polished)

1964-68 Novi 1200 carbureted
Mustang/Cougar/Comet/Falcon/Fairlane
260-302 driver-side mount, p/n 1001840
(satin), p/n 1001840-P (polished)

1969 Novi 1200 carbureted Mustang/Comet/Falcon/Fairlane 351W passenger-side mount,
p/n 1001843 (satin), p/n 1001843-P
(polished)

1969 Novi 1200 carbureted
Mustang/Cougar/Comet/Falcon/Fairlane
351W driver-side mount, p/n 1001844
(satin), p/n 1001844-P (polished)

Paxton Automotive Products, Inc.
1300 Beacon Place
Channel Islands, CA 93033-9901
1-888-9-PAXTON
Phone: (805) 487-3796
Fax: (805) 247-0669
www.paxtonauto.com

Paradise Paxton

Earlier in this chapter, we discussed Craig Conley from Paradise Paxton, a division of Paradise Wheels, Inc., who acquired the production rights and ownership of the Paxton SN-60 family. Conley and his staff are experts at rebuilding both the McCulloch VS Series and Paxton SN Series centrifugal blowers. They not only rebuild customer cores, but they also offer brand new, Paxton SN-60-Series kits for 289/302 engine Shelbys and Mustangs, as well as their SN-2000-based 1986-1993 5.0L kits.

"Our vintage street supercharger kits for the 1965-1968 Shelbys and Mustangs feature the classic Paxton SN-60 outer case with up-to-date SN-2000 internal components, so you basically get the best of both worlds," says Conley.

Also big news is Paradise Paxton's new Twin Paxton supercharger kit for 1965 to 1970 289/302 V-8s available in either two-stage, single 4-barrel applications, or straight blow-through dual-quad applications. Listed below are the kits Paradise Paxton offers. Since the product line is limited to a total of five (5) kits, there are no officially assigned part numbers.

1966-1967 SN-2000 carbureted kit for 289
Shelby GT350 and Mustang

1967-1970 SN-2000 carbureted kit for 289/302-
engine Shelby GT350 and Mustang

1986-1993 5.0L EFI Mustang LX and GT and
1993 SVT Mustang Cobra

1965-1970 two-stage, single-quad twin-super-
charger kit for Shelby/Mustang/Falcon/
Fairlane V-8s

1965-1970 straight blow-through dual-quad twin-
supercharger kit for Shelby/Mustang/
Falcon/Fairlane V-8s

Paradise Paxton
A division of Paradise Wheels, Inc.
920 Rancheros Drive, Unit "E"
San Marcos, CA 92069
Phone: (760) 740-0954
Fax: (760) 740-0956
Email: conleyr107@aol.com
www.paradisewheelsinc.com

Powerdyne Automotive Products, Inc.

Powerdyne Automotive Products, Inc. features their 50-state-legal BD-11A supercharger, which operates at a safe 6 to 9 psi. The silent-drive cog-belt-driven BD-11A is self-contained, self-lubricating, and is available for all 5.0L 1986-1993 Mustangs and all 1988-2005 V-8 light-duty trucks.

Also available is the company's Silent Drive BD-600 model, which is designed for smaller-displacement V-6 and V-8 engines, as well as for use in applications where space is at a premium. Mod-motor Mustang and F-Series enthusiasts will be happy to learn that Powerdyne's BD-11A and reverse-rotation BD-11AR are available in a number of applications for 1996-2005 cars and trucks.

Paradise Paxton offers a two-stage twin supercharger kit for the 1965-1970 model single 4-barrel-carbureted Mustangs. This kit features a pair of SN-60/SN2000 superchargers pumping out 10 to 14 psi.

1986-1993 Mustang 5.0L, 9 psi, BD-11A silent drive, p/n K-10179-101 (satin), p/n K-10179-201 (polished), requires fuel pump and computer upgrades

1993 5.0L SVT Mustang Cobra, 8 psi, BD-11A silent drive, p/n K-10193-101 (satin), p/n K-10193-201 (polished), includes FMU

1993 5.0L SVT Mustang Cobra, 9 psi, BD-11A silent drive, p/n K-10172-101 (satin), p/n K-10173-201 (polished), includes 190-lph electric in-tank pump, computer chip, and FMU

1986-1993 Mustang 5.0L, 9 psi, XB-1A gear drive, K-10173-102 (satin), p/n K-10173-201 (polished), 190-lph electric in-tank pump and computer chip

1986-1993 Mustang 5.0L, 12 psi, XB-1A gear drive, p/n K-10174-201 (satin), p/n K-10174-202 (polished), includes 255-lph electric in-tank fuel pump, aftermarket ignition upgrade, and 8-rib pulley setup

1986-1993 Mustang 5.0L, 12 psi, XB-1A gear drive, p/n K-10175-102 (satin), p/n K-10175-202 (polished), requires fuel pump and aftermarket ignition upgrades

1994-1995 Mustang 5.0L, 6 psi, BD-11A silent drive, p/n K-10177-101 (satin), p/n K-10177-201 (polished), includes FMU

1994-1995 Mustang 5.0L, 9 psi, BD-11A silent drive, p/n K-10178-101 (satin), p/n K-10178-201 (polished), includes 190-lph electric in-tank fuel pump and computer chip

1994-1995 Mustang 5.0L, 9 psi, BD-11A silent drive, p/n K-10176-101 (satin), p/n K-10176-201 (polished), requires fuel pump and computer upgrades

Paradise Paxton's 1965-1967 street blower kit is very similar to the original Paxton-Shelby GT 350 street blower kit listed as a factory option on the 289-powered 1966 Shelby GT 350s and Mustangs. The real difference here is the internal workings. Paradise Paxton retains the original outer appearance by using the blue Paxton SN-60 ball bearing drive outer case, but equips it with more reliable, up-to-date, SN-2000 internal components.

Powerdyne also manufactures their gear-driven XB-1A and XB-1A-R models for high-boost, high-horsepower applications. These blowers feature helical-cut gears, are externally lubricated, and can safely operate at boost levels up to 18 psi. Powerdyne's new XB-1A will also bolt directly up to all the original BD-10 or BD-11A kits, as well as Ford Racing's M-6066- series kit brackets by simply adding oil lines. Listed below are Powerdyne's Mustang applications.

1986-1993 Mustang 5.0L, 8 psi, BD-11A silent drive, p/n K10170-101 (satin), p/n K10170-201 (polished), includes FMU

1986-1993 Mustang 5.0L, 9 psi, BD-11A silent drive, p/n K10171-101 (satin), p/n K10171-201 (polished), includes 190-lph in-tank electric fuel pump and computer chip

This cutaway view of the oil-fed Powerdyne XB-1A Series blower clearly shows the unit's helical-cut gearbox. It is capable of producing up to 18 psi, and the XB-1A is also available in reverse rotation, the XB-1AR.

The 5.0L engine BD-11A Series Powerdyne street blower kits can be upgraded to the XB-1A-trim Powerdyne gear charger by simply swapping the blowers out (as shown on this 5.0L engine Mustang LX) and plumbing in a new oil feed line. This upgrade also applies to the FRT M-6066 Series street blower kits as well as the Powerdyne-manufactured B&M Automotive Products street blower kits.

1994-1995 Mustang 5.0L, 12 psi, XB-1A gear drive, p/n K-10180-102 (satin), p/n K-10180-202 (polished), includes 255-lph electric in-tank fuel pump, aftermarket ignition, 8-rib supercharger pulley, and bypass valve

1994-1995 Mustang Cobra 5.0L, 6 psi, BD-11A silent drive, p/n K-10195-101 (satin), p/n K-10195-201 (polished), includes FMU

1994-1995 Mustang Cobra 5.0L, 9 psi, BD-11A silent drive, p/n K-10186-101 (satin), p/n 10186-201 (polished), includes 190-lph electric in-tank fuel pump, computer chip, and FMU

1994-1995 Mustang 5.0L, 9 psi, XB-1A gear drive, p/n K-10178-102 (satin), p/n K-10178-202 (polished), includes 190-lph electric in-tank fuel pump and computer chip

1996-1997 Mustang 4.6L, 8 psi, BD-600 silent drive, p/n K-10190-101 (satin), p/n K-10190-201 (polished), includes 190-lph electric in-tank fuel pump

1998 Mustang 4.6L, 8 psi, BD-600 silent drive, p/n K10194-101 (satin), p/n K-10194-201 (polished), includes 200-lph in-line fuel pump

2000-2001 Mustang 4.6L, 8 psi, BD-11R silent drive, p/n K-10196-101 (satin), p/n K-10196-201 (polished), includes 36-lb/hr fuel injectors, 255-lph in-tank electric fuel pump, and custom-tuned computer chip

2001 Mustang Cobra 4.6L, 7 psi, XB-1A gear drive, p/n K-10197-101 (satin), p/n K-10197-202 (polished), includes 255-lph electric in-tank pump, FMU, computer chip, 38-lb/hr fuel injectors

2001 Mustang Cobra 4.6L, 7 psi, XB-1R gear drive, p/n K-10197-101 (satin), p/n K-10197-201 (polished), includes 36-lb/hr fuel injectors, 255-lph electric in-tank fuel pump, and custom-tuned computer chip

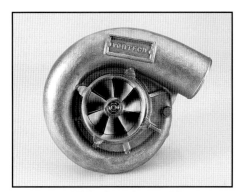

Vortech's "V" Series of gear-driven street superchargers began with the V-1A trim (shown here). The design has since evolved all the way up to the Vortech V-9 gear charger. Visit www.vortechsuperchargers.com for specific types, applications, and part numbers.

2005 Mustang 4.6L 3-valve, 6 psi, BD-11A silent drive, part numbers pending

4.6L/5.4L 3-valve trucks, part numbers pending

Powerdyne Automotive Products, Inc
A division of Wheeler Racing
104-C East Avenue K-4
Lancaster, CA 93535
Phone: (661) 723-2800
Fax: (661) 723-2802
www.Powerdyne.com

Vortech Engineering

Vortech Engineering's famed V-1A trim gear-driven centrifugal supercharger has won more Best Engineered and Best Product awards at the SEMA (Specialty Equipment Market Association) Show than any other street blower manufacturer in attendance.

Vortech's OE-type approach to system development is centered on the philosophy of safe boost design. This ensures the best blend of overall performance and reliability. Vortech superchargers produce more horsepower at a lower boost level than you might expect because of superior compressor efficiency and system configuration.

Vortech supercharger systems are 100 percent complete, allowing effortless installation for the experienced do-it-yourselfer. Shown here is the Renegade V-7YSi-Trim street/strip supercharger package, which can produce up to 1,000 hp. This kit is for off-road use only.

The original V-1A design has evolved into a total of 15 different trim types, or models, featuring different boost ranges:

V-1A-Trim, STD clockwise rotation.

V-1 S-Trim, STD/HD available counter-clockwise rotation.

V-1 SC-Trim, STD/HD clockwise rotation.

V-1 T-Trim, HD available clockwise or counter-clockwise rotation.

V-2 SQ E-Trim, STD, available clockwise or counter-clockwise rotation.

V-2 SQ S-Trim, STD, available clockwise or counter-clockwise rotation.

V-2 SQ SC-Trim, TD, available clockwise or counter-clockwise rotation.

V-4 J-Trim, HD, clockwise rotation.

V-4 XX-Trim, HD, available clockwise rotation.

V-4 Z-Trim, HD, available clockwise rotation.

V-5 G-Trim, STD/HD, available clockwise or counter-clockwise rotation.

V-7 YS-Trim, HD, clockwise rotation. This supercharger is also known as the Renegade, as it is used to compete on the NMRA and Fun Ford Weekend Series events.

V-9 F-Trim, STD, available clockwise or counter-clockwise rotation.

V-9 G-Trim, STD, available clockwise or counter-clockwise rotation.

The key to Vortech Engineering's overwhelming success is probably the fact that the company conducts a rigorous R&D program that includes street, trackside, and chassis and engine dyno testing. Heck, Vortech even has its own blower dyno!

Vortech also manufactures a complete line of After Coolers and Charge Coolers, which unlike intercoolers, are mounted in-between the supercharger and the throttle body. These units are reputed to drop the intake charge temperature by 40 to 60 percent!

Vortech's 4.6L DOHC Cobra Mod Motor application for the 1999-2000 models with aftercooler feature is capable of producing 436 hp and 422 ft-lbs of torque.

Vortech conducts an aggressive R&D program on all its street and competition blowers. The company even has its own blower dyno, which was a first in the centrifugal street supercharger industry.

Not surprisingly, the company offers kits for both street and strip. They are:

1999-2004 4.6L 2V GT H.O. with after-cooler, CARB E.O.# D-213-17
1996-1998 4.6L 2V GT H.O. with after-cooler, CARB E.O.# D-213-17
1986-1993 5.0L V-8 H.O. with after-cooler, CARB E.O.# D-213-17
1994-1998 3.8L V-6 Mustang, CARB E.O.# D213-17

1986-1993 5.0L Renegade Racing, non-certified
1994-1995 5.0L SVT Mustang Cobra, CARB E.O.# D-213-17
1993 5.0L Cobra with after-cooler, CARB E.O.# D-213-17
1999-2003 4.6L 4V SVT Mustang Cobra, CARB E.O.# D-213-17
2005 4.6L 3-valve Mustang GT, Reverse Rotation, CARB E.O. Pending.

Vortech Engineering, LLC
1650 Pacific Avenue
Channel Islands, CA 93022-9901
Phone: (805) 247-0226
Fax: (805) 247-0669
www.vortechsuperchargers.com

Above: Vortech Engineering's air-to-water aftercoolers (charge coolers) are reputed to lower the air intake charge up to 40 to 60 percent on FoMoCo mod motor or pushrod V-8s. Left: Vortech Engineering's Mondo competition supercharger package for the 5.0L and 5.8L pushrod V-8 engine Mustangs was designed for high-boost street-and-strip applications like bracket racing and competition at Fun Ford Weekend events. These kits are for off-road use only.

BUILDING A PAXTON-SUPERCHARGED 289 FORD "HI-PO" SMALL-BLOCK VINTAGE RACE ENGINE

The rumble is unmistakably Shelby – that whine is unmistakably Paxton! There's nothing sweeter than the melodious whine and throaty rumble of a Paxton-supercharged 289 Ford small-block engine. That's exactly how nightclub owner Fred Piluso felt after researching the history on his latest purchase, a black- and -gold 1966 Shelby GT-350-H, serial number SFM 1653.

"The car was originally an automatic transmission car, and (according to the Shelby World Registry) it was updated sometime in the early 1970s with a Paxton supercharger. The registry also reveals the fact that the car was extensively drag raced in the central Ohio area!"

However, by the time Piluso purchased SFM 1653, the blower was long gone, and so were the original 289 Hi-Po heads. The correct serial number Shelby aluminum factory intake manifold was still there, but the old "rent-a-racer" had the wrong Holley carburetor. To add insult to injury, just about everything else inside the engine compartment that was indicative of a genuine Shelby GT-350-H was also missing.

"The car was a real mess. Instead of the Hi-Po heads, it had a set of 2-barrel 302 heads. We ran a leak-down test on the old engine and discovered that the compression numbers were all over the chart," said Craig Conley of Paradise Paxton. "The installation of a supercharger on an engine like this would have been a disaster!"

Prior to installing a new Paxton SN-60 outer case equipped with up-to-date SN-2000 internal workings, Piluso wisely elected to have Craig Conley and the Paradise Paxton crew completely rebuild and blueprint the Shelby's 289 Hi-Po engine.

Conley continued, "Our objective was to build basically a good running blueprinted Paxton-supercharged 289 street engine capable of safely producing approximately around 375 horsepower on Supreme Unleaded pump gasoline. We wanted this

Selected for this build were a set of 0.010-inch Ross flat-top forged-aluminum free-floating pistons and a set of 2.100-inch-wide bearing Chevrolet journal Eagle H-beam forged-steel connecting rods equipped with ⁷⁄₁₆-inch ARP cap screw rod bolts. The final compression ratio on this engine should come in at around 9.5:1 to 10:1.

engine to be able to compete in either open track events or at the drags. And, we also wanted to keep things as original as possible (at least externally) so that the car could be shown at any Mustang or Shelby-related concourse.

"What we wanted to do here was maximize the Paxton's true performance potential. We did that through the cam and by performing a little bit of headwork while basically blueprinting the motor. Fortunately for us, the original 306-hp K-Code 289 Hi-Po block had never been rebuilt, and it was in excellent condition. All we had to do was come up with a set of 289 Hi-Po heads!"

When it came to the internal components for the engine, Conley selected the very best. That included ordering a set of

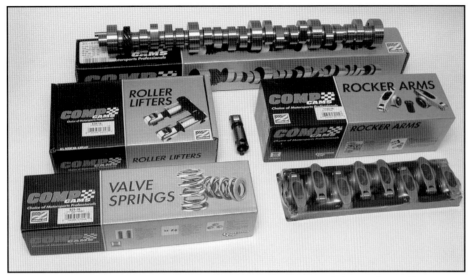

Paxton's Craig Conley and his crew selected a special grind Comp Cams flat tappet roller cam with a lobe center of 112-degrees, featuring an intake duration of 0.050 inch at 243 degrees, and an exhaust duration of 0.050-inch at 0.247 degrees. Also selected was a set of Comp Cams roller lifters, valve springs, 7.025-inch pushrods, and 1.6:1 ratio roller rocker arms.

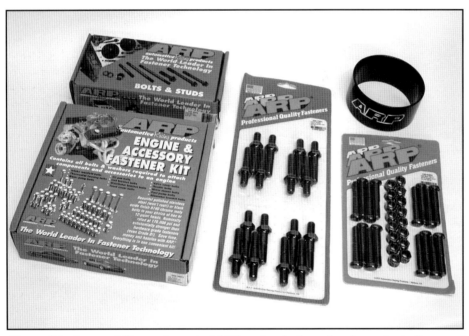

Also enlisted was a full complement of ARP engine fastener hardware, including a set of 7⁄16-inch ARP head and main studs, an ARP engine and accessory fastener kit, ARP 7⁄16-inch rocker arm set, ARP piston ring compressor, and ARP oil pan bolt kit. The ARP damper bolt and flywheel bolt kit are not shown.

.010-inch overbore Ross forged-aluminum flat-top pistons (approximate compression ratio of 9.1:1), along with a set of wide bearing Chevy-journal Eagle H-beam forged-steel connecting rods featuring 7⁄16-inch ARP rod bolts. The engine features a Competition Cams mechanical roller cam (grind #31-000-9) that's tolerable for the street, yet features a wide enough lobe center (112-degrees, 243-degrees intake duration at 0.050, 247 degrees exhaust duration at 0.050) to be able to breathe and work in conjunction with the Paxton supercharger. The valvetrain also includes Comp Cams flat-tappet roller lifters, 7.025-inch Comp Cams pushrods, Comp Cams valvesprings, Ferrea stainless-steel 1.94/1.60-inch intake and exhaust valves, and a set of Comp Cams 1.6:1-ratio roller rocker arms for 0.556 inches of valve lift.

The buildup also included a 650-cfm Holley 4-barrel carburetor and a set of Doug's Headers Tri-Y headers. Since the Shelby was being converted over to a 4-speed, it needed a McLeod bell housing, a Centerforce lightweight billet-aluminum flywheel, and a Dual Friction clutch.

Engine Block and Rotating Assembly

"When building a supercharged engine such as this, you want to maximize the thickness of the cylinder walls to maintain the overall integrity of the block and get maximum durability out of the engine. So, less cubic inches are better."

Since Piluso's K-Code 289 Hi-Po engine block had never been rebuilt, a 0.010-inch cleanup bore with a deck plate was all that was necessary. In the process, the crew at Paradise Paxton also stress-relieved and de-burred the block, and had it hot tanked and sonic cleaned. Then the block was line honed and decked to square it up to the center of the crank.

Next, the 289 Hi-Po crank was ground to 0.010 inch on the mains and 0.020 inch on the rod journals. In the process, the crank was Magnafluxed and de-burred, and the oil holes were chamfered. With all of the machine work done, the re-awakened 289 Hi-Po was externally balanced with a 28-ounce balancer.

Upon assembly, the torque specs on the mains will be set at 85 ft-lbs, working from the center main out.

"We basically set the main bearing clearance to racing specifications (0.0025-0.0030 inch), since this engine is going to be run pretty hard. Rod journal clearances were set at around 0.0025 to 0.0026 inch, with a side-to-side clearance of 0.016 to 0.019 inch.

"Because this is a supercharged engine, the piston ring gap on the Childs and Albert chrome-moly piston rings was left a little loose, at 0.020 and 0.025 inch. Piston-to-wall clearance was also loosely set following Ross recommended clearance of 0.005 to 0.007 inch. Upon assembly, the

Also included in the build was the correct specification Holley HLYO-80674 650-cfm four-barrel carburetor.

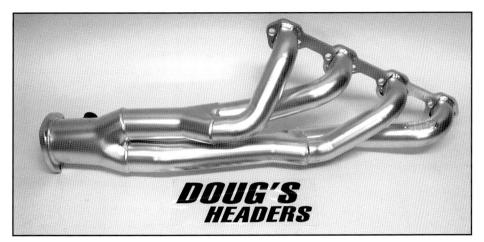

The folks at Doug's Headers also came to the party with a set of their thermal-barrier-coated DTE-289Y Tri-Y headers, which are direct reproductions of the original Shelby factory Tri-Y tubular headers.

Hi-Po cylinder head machine work included a new three-angle valve job and installing new bronze valve guides. Modifications included opening up the bowl on the exhaust side of the head and modifying the short-term radius on the exhaust port. The exhaust port was also maximized using the Fel-Pro exhaust gasket as a template.

connecting rod bolts were final-torqued to 70 ft-lbs.

"Again, being that this was a super-charged engine, deck height was set a little low as well (0.007 inch), giving us an acceptable piston-to-head clearance using the Fel-Pro 'blue' head gasket.

"One of the things that we did was install a Boss 302 windage tray and a Melling Performance standard volume oil pump. The engine runs 20W-40W Royal Purple Racing oil through a K&N High Performance Gold oil filter and original Shelby GT-350 T-oil pan."

Cylinder Head Preparation

"We also did quite a bit of work to the Hi-Po 289 heads. After completely disassembling them, they were Magnafluxed and completely de-burred. Then we sent them over to Greg Grosset at Total Performance where he performed a 3-angle valve job and installed a new set of bronze liners.

"When we got the heads back, we performed what you would call a 'supercharged porting job,' which favors the exhaust side of the head. That included opening up the bowl on the exhaust valve. We also achieved a nice, short turn radius on the exhaust port, and opened the exhaust port up to its maximum limit, using the Fel-Pro gasket as a guide.

"We also cleaned up the bowl in the intake port, and once again matched the size of the intake port to the Fel-Pro gasket. Combustion chamber volume wound up being a total of 57 cc.

"We didn't want to kill too much of the bottom-end torque and performance with the supercharged engine by going to too low of a compression. A factory Hi-Po 289 is 10:1 compression stock. With the supercharger, 9:1 compression is ideal. But since Hawaii has such great (dense) air and the car will be running high octane fuel, the final compression ratio turned out to be a calculated 9.932:1!"

Induction System and Supercharger

Since this is a resto-rod application, installation of the Paradise Paxton SN-60-SN 2000 6-psi supercharger was basically textbook. However, some things were done

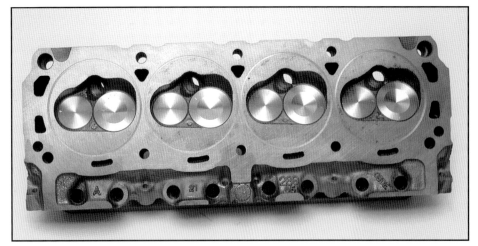

Other than customary polishing, combustion chamber modifications were minor. Once completed, the technicians at Paradise Paxton installed a 1.90-inch intake valve and 1.60-inch Ferrea stainless-steel exhaust valve.

Just prior to final assembly, combustion chamber volume is checked, and it specs out at a total of 57 cc.

1. Short-block buildup begins with installation of the Comp Cams flat tappet roller cam using plenty of assembly lube. "When we installed the cam bearings, we restricted the oil hole opening running to the cam bearing down to 0.060 inch. This is a little trick we do to all the 289 Ford engines because they have too large an oil hole running to the cam bearings, which winds up bleeding off a lot of the oil that could go to the connecting rods and main bearings," says Craig Conley.

2. With Clevite engine bearings already installed, liberal amounts of engine assembly lube is applied to the main bearings.

3. The fully prepared 289 Hi-Po crankshaft goes in. Torque is set at 85 ft-lbs in increments of 25, 50, and 80 ft-lbs, working from the center out.

to the 650-cfm Holley carburetor and Shelby factory 4V intake that bear mentioning.

"First we port-matched the intake ports on the manifold to match those on the 289 Hi-Po cylinder heads," said Conley. "Then we installed a 6.5-lb power valve inside the Holley, along with installing a number-73 Jet in the primary fuel block and a number-88 jet in the secondary fuel block. We also installed a set of solid nitrophyl fuel floats to prevent the floats from collapsing under full boost conditions."

When it came to the Shelby's ignition system, Conley and company upgraded the factory Ford dual-point distributor with a Pertronix Igniter electronic setup set at 16-degrees initial timing, and a total of 34- to 36-degrees total advance.

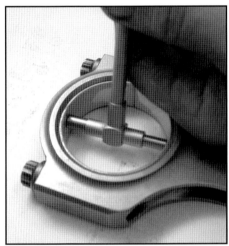

4. The rod bolts are torqued to 65 ft-lbs. Then the inner and outer dimension of crank throw and connecting rod bearing are checked.

5. Next, the Childs & Albert file-to-fit top ring gap is checked and a measurement of 0.020 to 0.025 inch is achieved.

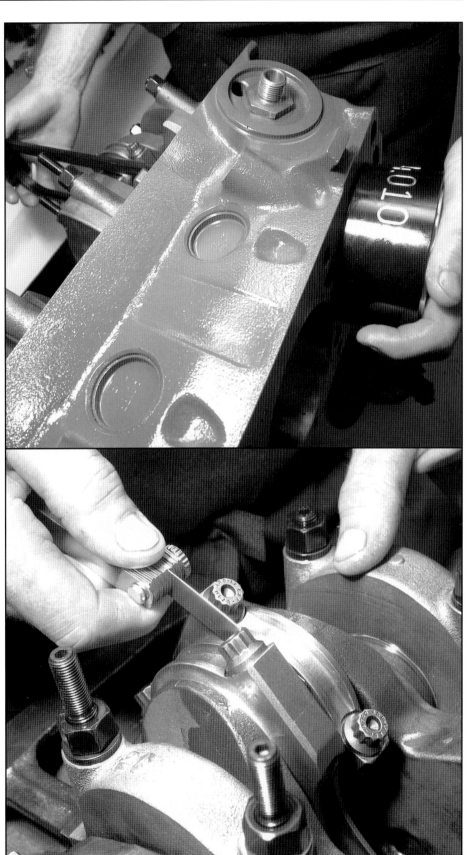

6. In go the completed (Eagle) rod and (Ross) piston assemblies using the ARP piston ring compressor. Final torque on the ⁷⁄₁₆-inch ARP rod bolts is set at 65 ft-lbs of torque.

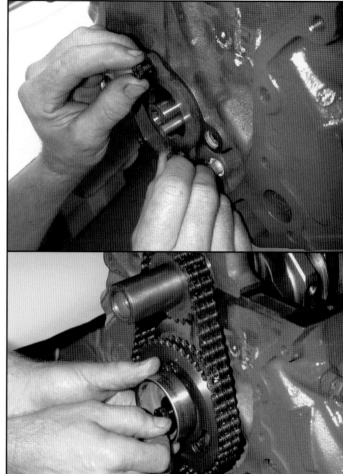

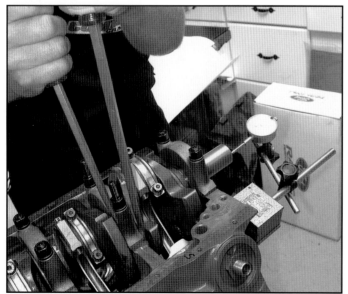

8. With the crank, rod, and piston assemblies both planted, the cam plate and Cloyes Tru-Roller multiple index timing chain are installed.

7. Crankshaft end-thrust is set using a large pair of screwdrivers. Side-to-side connecting rod clearance is checked and gives a reading of 0.016 to 0.017 inch.

9. A Comp Cams degree wheel is used to dial in the cam, which is set at 2 to 3 degrees advance.

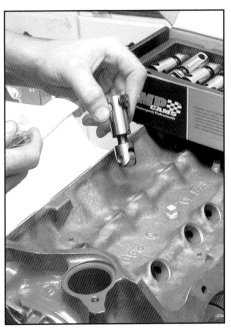

12. With the block flipped back over, it's time to install the Comp Cams roller lifters using plenty of assembly lube.

10. Our builder installs the Melling Performance standard volume oil pump and FRT Boss 302 windage tray using ARP hardware.

11. Of course, this is followed with installing the original Shelby American T-oil pan using the ARP oil pan bolts provided in the ARP Engine Hardware kit.

13. The 289 Hi-Po heads are installed over the ARP head studs and torqued to 85 ft-lbs, working from the center out.

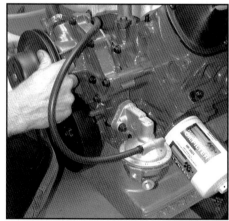

16. The Pertronix-Ignitor-equipped Ford distributor is installed using the provided ARP distributor bolt and factory hold down. When the system is final-tuned, it is set at 34 to 36 degrees total advance.

14. Next comes installing the Comp Cams roller rocker arms. Valve lash is set at 0.016 inch intake and 0.018 inches exhaust.

15. Next comes installing the port-matched Shelby aluminum intake using the ARP intake manifold bolts torqued to 25 ft-lbs.

17. Blower installation begins with installation of the Paradise Paxton heavy-duty fuel pump.

18. One of Paradise Paxton's technicians trial-fits the two-piece cast-aluminum blower box to the intake

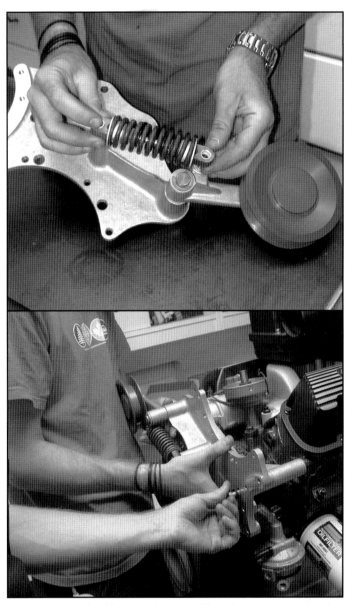

19. Next comes installing the Paxton belt crank pulley using a total of three 3/8-inch bolts provided in the kit.

20. Setting up the idler tensioner and bracket comes next using the ⅜ x 6-inch long bolts, which bolt up to the head, and two ⁵⁄₁₆-inch bolts, which secure the bracket to the water pump.

21. The Paxton air box and Holley carburetor are bolted down using four ⁵⁄₁₆-inch studs.

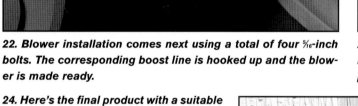

22. Blower installation comes next using a total of four 5/16-inch bolts. The corresponding boost line is hooked up and the blower is made ready.

23. Prior to installing the clamshell top of the air box, the carburetor throttle linkage is hooked up and tested. The lid is then permanently bolted on.

24. Here's the final product with a suitable recipient waiting in the wings!

INSTALLING PAXTON NOVI 1000 ON A 4.6L MUSTANG GT

The Novi 1000 is Paxton's entry-level gear-driven street supercharger package. However, that's not to imply that the 50-state-legal Paxton Novi 1000 lacks the same "umph" of its bigger brothers, the Novi 2000 and the race-bred Novi 3000. What that means is that the Novi 1000 was designed to appeal to performance enthusiasts who want the power of a centrifugal supercharger in a compact package – and that's the Novi 1000 in spades!

The Novi 1000 features a wide boost range that enables it to be used on either 4 or 6-cylinder inline engines, as well as small-displacement V-6 and V-8 engines. That means at approximately 281 ci, a bone-stock version of Ford's 4.6L two-valve engine is *the* perfect candidate.

The 4.6-liter Mustang requires a reverse-rotation bower. Due to the close proximity of the related engine systems components on the 4.6L SOHC Ford modular V-8 engine and its relatively large dimensions, it became necessary for Paxton engineers to invert the supercharger. The 500-hp Novi 1000 is mounted to a sturdy two-piece, billet-aluminum cradle mounting bracket. Of course, that doesn't affect the performance any, it just makes everything fit like factory.

Aside from the trick cradle-style supercharger mounting bracket, this particular kit also includes a set of cast-aluminum air discharge tubes, a set of 30 lb/hr fuel injectors, a programmed computer chip, a K&N lifetime conical air filter, a Paxton air bypass, and a Paxton anti-surge valve. The kit comes with an assortment of flex-hose elbows and air ducting, an eight-rib replacement serpentine accessory drive belt, all the necessary nuts and bolts, and above all, a fully detailed 30-page installation book.

What kind of performance numbers can your average Mustang enthusiast expect (that is, if there is such a person) with a Novi 1000 kit? On the Paxton

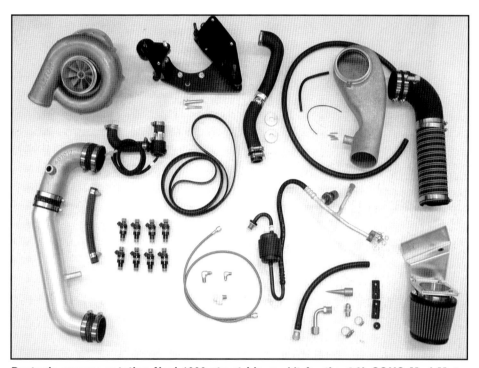

Paxton's reverse-rotation Novi 1000 street blower kit for the 4.6L SOHC Mod Motor Mustang comes complete with virtually every component needed to transform your docile 2-valve into a street stormer, minus factory re-configured computer chip

dyno, this Rio Red 2001 Mustang GT convertible produced a best of 220.4 hp at 5,250 rpm and 252.5 ft-lbs of torque at 4,250 rpm in naturally aspirated trim.

After the installation of the reverse rotation Paxton Novi 1000, the horsepower increased to a best of 389.7 hp at 5,750 rpm and 375.4 ft-lbs at 4,750 rpm. That's roughly a 77 to 78 percent increase in maximum horsepower, with a corresponding 49 percent increase in peak torque!

Paxton also offers this kit with an after-cooler, which is capable of raising the horsepower quotient from the stock 260 hp to 436 hp, with a gain of 120 ft-lbs of torque. The after-cooler kit is CARB certified, too.

However, there is one fly in the ointment that may scare away certain would-be Novi 1000 installers whose late-model Mustang is their only source

of transportation. You either have to get a custom computer chip burned, or send your computer to Paxton for upgrades, depending on your model of Mustang. This will probably mean at least a little bit of downtime.

Other than that, Paxton Automotive's Novi 1000 supercharger kit is fairly straightforward. Of course, you'll need an assortment of SAE and metric hand tools (mostly metric), along with a ⅜-inch x 18 NPT pipe tap, a floor jack (or better yet, a lift), a set of jack stands, and, of course, a supply of buckets or catch cans to collect and reuse that expensive coolant. Paxton Automotive Products also recommends obtaining a Helms Publications 2001 Mustang Shop Manual for those in doubt.

Now follow along with us as a Paxton technician performs his magic on this 2001 Mustang GT convertible.

1. Disassembly begins with disconnecting the plastic crankcase breather hose and air idle bypass hose from the stock 4.6L air intake system.

2. Next comes removing the air temperature sensor and mass airflow sensors from the factory air intake hose. These factory sensors are reused with the Paxton Novi 1000-RR street blower kit.

3. The Paxton Mass Airflow Sensor/screen assembly is then set up, transferring both factory sensor and screen to the Paxton housing and bracket. This unit is then set aside for later installation.

4. Vehicle teardown continues by removing the four 10-mm bolts securing the OE water pump pulley. The 4.6L accessory drive belt is also removed.

5. A 13-mm socket is used to remove the idler pulley located above the serpentine belt tensioner. The pulley is set aside and reused later. In the process, our installer also removed the two 13-mm timing cover bolts and 10-mm alternator mounting bolts at the front of the engine.

6. The Paxton Novi 1000 RR gear charger idler pulley bracket and the Ford factory idler pulley are installed onto the front of the 4.6L 2-valve modular V-8 engine using the supplied hardware.

7. The factory Ford idler pulley is reinstalled using the factory mounting hardware, followed by installing the Novi 1000-RR supercharger idler pulley. The supercharger rear bracket support is then installed, using the special 10-mm-long bolt provided. Leave it loose; it is necessary to move around the bracket in order to install the main supercharger support cradle bracket.

8. The main supercharger support cradle bracket is bolted up, installing the two ⅜-inch bolts and spacers in the upper portion of the bracket. Next, the lower-most bolt is installed using the two spacers provided, one in-between the brackets and one in between the 4.6L SOHC cylinder head. The stock 4.6L accessory drive belt is then reinstalled.

9. Paxton Novi 1000-RR installation requires the replacement of the factory Ford 24 lb/hr electronic fuel injectors with 30 lb/hr Paxton units. Our installer removes the two 8-mm bolts on both ends of the 4.6L fuel rails and lifts them out. He then replaces the OE parts with the Paxton 30-pounders.

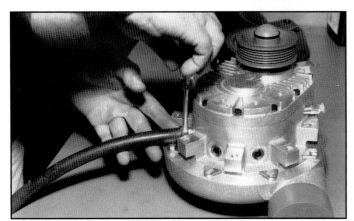

10. Supercharger setup begins with installing the oil drain back hose on the Novi 1000-RR supercharger unit. The hose clamp and screw head should be parallel to the supercharger mounting hose.

11. After removing the drive belt from the alternator pulley, the Novi 1000-RR gear charger is installed onto the main bracket. Once the supercharger is installed, it can be fully tightened, the belt tensioner can be released, and the accessory drive belt can be installed back in place.

12. Now comes the critical oil feed and drain line procedure. It should be noted that our installer has already done the hard work. That requires setting up the 90-degree factory oil sending unit into the provided Paxton brass junction fitting. A location hole is marked at the front of the oil pan, and a ⅛-inch pilot hole is drilled using either a magnetic drill bit or one covered with heavy grease to trap all the metal chips. After applying a little Anti-Seize to the punch, the necessary opening is made using the ⅜-inch NPT tap, and the fitting is summarily installed.

14. The length of supplied rubber hose is hooked up to the hard crank case ventilation line that runs from the drivers-side valve cover across the 4.6L two-valve engine. This hose is routed over the passenger-side valve cover and runs toward the front of the GT's 4.6L SOHC modular V-8 engine.

13. The Paxton Novi 1000-RR intake tract is now set up. The supplied Novi 1000-RR supercharger discharge tube assembly is mounted as shown, using the supplied rubber hoses and clamps.

15. The idle air control valve is joined to the 4.6L throttle body housing reusing the original factory hose. It is then re-routed to the air discharge tube via the supplied length of rubber hose and hose clamps provided in the kit.

16. The supercharger bypass valve also requires a vacuum source. The existing plastic vacuum fitting that runs along the firewall on the passenger side is removed and replaced with a plastic vacuum T fitting. One end is attached to the supplied length of vacuum hose and routed along the passenger-side frame rails toward the supercharger. It is connected to the bypass valve assembly later on.

17. The new Paxton Automotive MAF is relocated to the inside of the inner passenger fender well. A hydraulic lift is used to make the work easier. The Paxton MAF/air filter bracket is placed over the existing studs, securing them in place using the original 10-mm nuts retained from the stock assembly.

18. The flex hose running from the new MAF assembly to the secondary intake tube is installed next.

19. With secondary intake tune and bypass valve assembly attached to the underside, installation is nearly complete. In the process, the oil feed line is installed and tightened to the Paxton Novi 1000-RR gear charger.

20. We covered installing the special Paxton OBD II legal chip in the body copy of our text. Here we see our man doing the deed.

21. With the Novi 1000-RR supercharged engine running, a series of visual checks is performed. Then it's time to go to the dyno room. Results show a 77 to 78 percent increase in max horsepower at 5,750 rpm, and a 49 percent increase in max torque at 4,750 rpm; and that's without one of Paxton's aftercooler units installed.

BUILDING AN AF-FORD-ABLE 408-CI RENEGADE WINDSOR V-8

The proof is in the dyno numbers. Many dream about building an affordable supercharged small-block Ford V-8, but more than likely, very few actually go out and do it for fear that it will: A) Be prohibitively expensive and require a ton of exotic and costly high-performance aftermarket parts or B) once the job's done, the darn thing won't even be close to being streetable.

Yeah, well, dig this. What would you say if we told you that you could build a storming 408-ci Ford "small-block" (ah, hem!) that'll produce gobs of horsepower, can be driven on the street, and will cost in the neighborhood of 10 to 12K? Have we got your attention?

"An engine like this should be capable of producing between 450 and 475 streetable horsepower naturally aspirated," said Dennis Hilliard, from Tehachapi, California's Central Coast Motorsports (CCM). "And, once coupled up to a Vortech V-7YSi-Trim Renegade supercharger, this same combination will produce approximately 700 to 750 safe horsepower with around 650 to 700 ft-lbs of torque!"

And what kind of a car would you put something like that in? Any car you want, really. Seriously though, one of the hottest classes at the Fun Ford Weekend Series of drag racing events is their True Street category.

"In order to successfully compete in this class, you can run any combination of engine just as long as it's in a fully licensed, street-legal car, competing on any size DOT drag radial tire you can fit underneath the fender well," says Fun Ford Weekend Technical Inspector George Klass.

Dennis Hilliard was quick to agree, "When installed in the right car (preferably a lightweight Mustang LX), an engine like that should put you solidly in the high 9s at over 140 mph!

"What I would recommend is that you use across-the-counter parts to

keep the cost at a respectable minimum. Once you get that combination dialed in, you can start pushing the envelope with custom cylinder head porting, larger-size fuel injectors, an exotic intake, and things like that. But for the time being, I would suggest that you maintain a conservative approach!" Hilliard definitely had our attention, but we still needed a little more convincing.

"With this kind of engine, I would suggest a later model Ford 351W engine block, a set of Ford Racing's new Canfield-produced M-6049-Z304 aluminum cylinder heads, a Crane Cams roller cam and valvetrain, and a Probe Industries 4340 forged-steel stroker crank and engine kit."

By now, we're quite certain that you're thinking, yeah, but what would one of these thumpers cost to build? "There's nothing trick about this engine. Any experienced mechanic can duplicate

what we're about to do here. And all of the parts are available through CCM. To duplicate this engine in long-block form, complete with fully outfitted FRT Z-304 heads and Probe Industries 408-ci stroker kit, you're looking at a cost of over $5,000. Of course, that's without the Vortech V-7YSi-Trim Renegade supercharger package, which would probably run you another $4,500!"

Probe Industries 408-ci Stroker Kit

As previously mentioned, the Probe Industries 408 stroker kit features a 4340 forged-steel, cross-drilled crank with a 4-inch stroke and a 4.30-inch bore. Since this engine will be supercharged, our builder recommended a set of standard-size 3-inch chamfered main bearings manufactured by a quality manufacturer like Childs & Albert over an OE-type main bearing.

Probe Industries' 4340 cross-drilled forged-steel crankshaft for the Ford 351W features a 4-inch stroke. When combined with a 4.030-inch bore, it yields a whopping 408-ci.

A set of 4340 forged-steel Eagle H-beam connecting rods, measuring 6.2 inches in length and outfitted with 7/16-inch ARP cap screw rod bolts and 8.9:1 compression SRP forged-aluminum dual spiro-lock pistons, make up the rest of the Pro Industries 408-ci 351 Windsor stroker engine kit.

Quality bearings will have superior lubricating properties, and their softer bearing surfaces are more capable of withstanding the brutal pounding delivered by a supercharged engine. A set of 4340 forged-steel 6.2-inch Eagle H-beam connecting rods and a set of 28-oz SRP forged-aluminum pistons ride on the stroker crank. This entire engine assembly comes fully balanced by West Valley Engine Balancing.

Selecting a Suitable 351W Engine Block

We selected a new old stock (NOS) '85 Ford 351W engine block that CCM had in stock.

"Any 351W engine block will do," said Dennis. "However, since this engine will feature a Crane roller cam, you will also need to order a set of Crane's 302/351W roller lifters. On the other hand, you may want to use the factory 351W roller cam block and roller lifter assembly, manufactured from 1994 to 1996, although the likelihood of finding one of those these days is kind of rare."

Machining Procedures

As far as machining the actual block, the block was sent out to be decked by CCM, and its cylinders were bored and honed (0.025-inch over bore with a 0.005-inch finish hone) to achieve an overall bore increase of 0.030 inches. Due to the superior clamping force of the ARP main studs, the main webs of the block were also line honed to maintain concentricity.

Other modifications included short filling our 351W with Moroso Block Filler to strengthen and stabilize the bottom portion of the cylinder wall, without incurring any unnecessary heating problems. The front oil passage galleys were also drilled and tapped using NPT oil galley plugs.

With some stroker kits, providing sufficient thrust-side crank clearance on the bottom end is a must. Initial mockup of the Probe Industries stroker crank did, however, reveal a few minor problem areas. CCM engine builder Paul Williams noted that, "We discovered that the rear flange on the crankshaft rubbed against the recess area on the block. This necessitated setting the block up in a line boring machine, taking a cutting tool, and clearancing the recess about 0.0060 inch.

"After mocking up the number-one rod and piston assembly, we also discovered that the oil pump mounting boss needed to be ground slightly to clear the number-one counterweight on the crankshaft."

With 700 to 750 hp on tap, does this engine need a girdle?

"Although many people prefer to use some type of engine girdle in applications like this, there's really no need since the 351W has plenty of 'beef' in the bottom end of the block," said Hilliard.

When it comes to providing adequate lubrication, you're definitely going to want to run a windage tray of some type.

Selected as the foundation for this buildup is an NOS 1988 Ford 351W roller cam block. Virtually any year 351 Windsor V-8 engine block (with minor modifications) can be used in this buildup. But since we are using a roller cam, we elected to make things easier (and less expensive) by finding a roller cam 351W engine block.

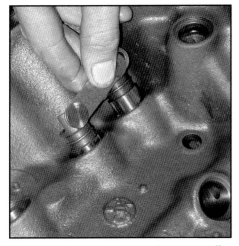

When running a roller cam in a non-roller cam block, it's necessary to run a set of Crane roller lifters.

"We're probably going to use one of FRT's M-6687-A351 units, along with an FRT M-6675-F3511 5-quart oil pan and Engine Tech Oil Pump, and a Ford Power Parts 351W steel billet oil pump driveshaft."

Selecting the Ideal Roller Camshaft

As previously mentioned, CCM selected a Crane Power Max hydraulic roller cam for this buildup. Cam characteristics feature 222 degrees duration and

0.552 inch max valve lift on the intake side, and 230 degrees duration and 0.574 inch max valve lift on the exhaust.

"This cam should make excellent power all the way up to 6,500 rpm," said Hilliard. "It looks like we have a lobe separation of approximately 112 degrees (meaning more exhaust overlap, which is necessary for a healthy breathing supercharged engine), which makes the Crane Power Max an ideal blower camshaft."

At this juncture, it should also be noted that Crane provides two dowel pins with this camshaft. The longer dowel pin is to be used on 1973 to 1979 351W engines, while the shorter dowel pin is to be used in 1980 and newer 351W engine blocks because of a different timing cover and face of the later-model Windsor blocks.

Ford Racing's Z-304 Cylinder Heads & Valvetrain Components

Ford Racing Technologies M-6049-Z304 heads are manufactured from A356 T-6-aluminum alloy and represent the very latest street/competition cylinder head technology. Weighing in at just 27 lbs apiece, these heads feature high-flow 204-cc intake ports, 85-cc exhaust ports,

and 64-cc combustio[n] bare and ready for f[ ] suggested valve size is intake side and 1.6[ ] exhaust. You should also use manganese-bronze valve guides and stainless-steel hardened seats.

The Z head also uses ⅜-inch screw-in rocker-arm studs with laser-cut pushrod guide plates. They can accept either tapered-seal or gasket-style 14-mm (we chose Denso Iridium) spark plugs, and feature not one, but two pair of exhaust manifold mounting holes drilled into the exhaust side of the head, allowing you to run numerous header combinations.

Airflow numbers are quite impressive. The intake flows a full 277.3 cfm at 0.550 inch of valve lift, and the exhaust checks in at 218.12 at 0.550 inch, making these heads heavy breathers to say the least.

When it came to selecting the proper valvetrain hardware, CCM lined up some fairly impressive equipment including a set of Manley 2.02-inch and 1.60-inch stainless-steel intake and exhaust valves, along with a set of Crane Cams 1.6:1 roller-rocker arms and dual valvesprings. Finally, a set of lightweight Ground Pounder sheetmetal aluminum valve covers was selected to protect all the goodies!

Extrude Honing our 408 Stroker's GT40/Cobra Intake System

Since we wanted to maximize airflow and keep cost down, we selected Ford Racing 351W GT40 cast-aluminum EFI lower intake manifolds and Cobra upper intake plenums. Recently, an aerospace industry-derived process known as "abrasive flow machining" has been applied to automotive induction and exhaust systems with tremendous success. Extrude Hone AFM is the industry leader in this field, and we've witnessed dramatic improvements in 5.0L and 5.8L induction systems after a trip to Extrude Hone.

We trucked our GT40/Cobra intake system over to Extrude Hone where technician Eddie Melendez bolted the system onto the company's Super Flow computerized airflow bench to establish a baseline. While the GT40 inherently flowed better than a stock 351W EFI intake system, we needed as much airflow improvement as we could get.

"Ideally, we're going to need to get at least 30 percent more cfm out of this system in order to realize this engine's true performance potential," replied Dennis Hilliard. As it turned out, we wouldn't be disappointed!

"Basically the amount of material we removed through the Extrude Hone abrasive flow machining process was approximately 1 to 1.5 mm per port," exclaimed Extrude Hone president Ed Melendez.

"Obviously, more material was removed in areas where there was greater restriction and resistance. Special emphasis was placed on intake ports one and five, and they were equalized to match the remaining ports."

After a couple of hot laps on the Extrude Hone abrasive flow machine, technician Eddie Melendez strapped our intake back on to his flow bench, and documented an average of 39 percent overall flow gain.

Last, but certainly not least, we selected one of Ground Pounder Performance Products' adjustable venturi, 65- to 75-mm billet-aluminum throttle bodies anodized in black.

The Vortech V-7YSi-Trim Supercharger

The oil-fed Vortech V-7YSi-Trim gear-driven centrifugal supercharger is capable of producing up to 20 psi using an 8-rib, 3-inch Renegade pulley (2.85-inch and 3.15-inch under-drive and over-drive pulleys are also available).

This blower kit features twin-aluminum supercharger mounting plates for increased rigidity and a 4-inch idler pulley with beefy mounting flanges. This new bracket assembly will also accept an optional second idler pulley on the belt tensioner side, should the customer choose to run a dual idler pulley system.

This unit features a 4-inch-diameter air inlet, with a 3.64-inch inducer on the supercharger. Maximum efficient impeller speed on this unit is 60,000 rpm

FRT's Canfield-produced M-6049-Z304 alloy cylinder heads are the perfect complement for our 408-ci Windsor stroker. Featuring the very latest in casting technology, these heads are manufactured from A356 T6 aluminum alloy and weigh a mere 27 lbs apiece. More importantly, they flow like gangbusters right out of the box – 227.3 cfm on the intake at 0.550-inch max valve lift, and 218.1 cfm on the exhaust at 0.550-inch max valve lift. These heads feature 64-cc combustion chambers manganese bronze valveguides, and stainless-steel hardened valve seats, making them ready for a three-angle street-and-strip valve job.

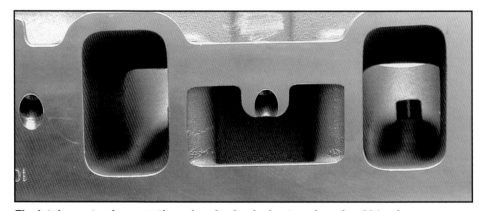

The intake port volume on these heads checks in at a whopping 204 cc!

with a 65,000-rpm redline. Max boost for the Vortech V-7YSi-Trim is 29 psi, and its adiabatic efficiency is 74 percent. For this buildup, we also selected a set of Vortech Engineering anodized fuel rails.

Support Hardware

For this build the folks at CCM chose a set of MSD 65-lb/hr fuel injectors, an MSD Flying Magnet Crank Trigger ignition setup (which gets its name because of the four magnets that are imbedded into the surface of the alu-minum crank trigger wheel attached to the harmonic balancer), an MSD Pro Billet 351W distributor, along with optional bronze distributor drive gear (an absolute must-have with a roller cam), and a Fuel Air Spark Technologies (F.A.S.T.) Electronic Engine Management System equipped with the company's C-Comp software. Other components include an Edelbrock high-flow aluminum reverse-rotation 5.0L/5.8L water pump, a Ford Racing heavy-duty clutch and pressure plate, and a 24-oz billet flywheel.

That pretty much covers our 351W-based, supercharged 408-ci stroker's equipment inventory. Noted engine builder Paul Williams conducted actual engine assembly in two phases. The 351W was mocked-up to trial fit all the components and check critical engine clearances. The engine was then final assembled and delivered to the dyno shop.

It's Time to Make Some Thunder!

On the dyno at Westech Performance Group, dyno tech Tom Habrzyk immediately began preparing our 408 for a trip to the "polygraph room," a humorous term the staff at Westech use to describe their Super Flow 901-equipped dyno cell. First, Habrzyk filled the crankcase of our 351 with 5 quarts of Royal Purple 10W-30 racing oil, and used a drill motor to run up the oil pressure, which pegged in at 68 lbs.

The next order of business was checking out the 408's fuel and ignition systems, followed by actually installing the engine on the dyno. In the process, Habrzyk fashioned all the necessary supercharger air ducting using various lengths of 3-½-inch aluminum tubing joined together with hose clamps and neoprene rubber hoses. Prior to firing the engine for the first time, the final step included installing a fresh set of Denso Iridium spark plugs.

Engine break-in was done for approximately 45 minutes on Union 76 92-octane pump gas at 20 degrees advance. Then Habrzyk and fellow dynamometer technician Steve Brule winged the big-inch Windsor engine for the first time in naturally aspirated trim. After a few fuel/air curve adjustments, here's what they achieved:

Max Engine Torque: 559.9 ft-lbs at 3,500 rpm

Max Horsepower: 455 hp at 4,900 rpm

Naturally aspirated, the 408 would make a very nice street engine, but our dyno technicians wondered out loud just how stout this combination might be with a more aggressive cam profile.

Unfortunately, we did experience one minor problem early on in the test-

The exhaust port volume checks in at 85 cc. Note the dual-header bolt pattern drilled into the surface of the head. It's ideal for swapping out header combinations either in the dyno room or at the track.

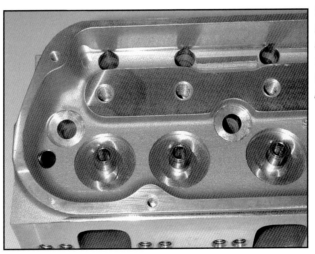

These heads also utilize ⅜-inch screw-in rocker arm studs using a set of ARP's 134-7104 rocker arm studs, which come with their own pushrod guide plates.

ing. With as much oil pressure as this engine has, a single oil breather was insufficient, and we were experiencing blow by. Oil baffling and adding an additional breather is the most obvious cure to the problem. However, since dyno time is golden time, the addition of an Accu-Sump oil reservoir evacuation system immediately took care of the problem.

After giving the engine a thorough check out, Brule and Habrzyk slapped on a new 8-rib serpentine belt, reinstalled all the maze of ducting to the blower, poured in some 100-octane

Rocker brand unleaded race gas, reset the timing at 20 degrees advance, and we were ready to rumble. In supercharged configuration, this is what we achieved on the first pull:

Max Engine Torque: 755.1 ft-lbs at 4,300 rpm

Max Horsepower: 707 hp at 5,300 rpm

Now we were getting somewhere! These numbers were produced at 12.3 lbs of boost. Obviously, the torque and horsepower increases over the naturally aspirated figures are quite significant. But we knew that there was still a little

The full complement of valvetrain components for this setup includes Crane Cams 1.6:1 ratio roller rocker arms, a set of Crane Cams triple valvesprings, a set of ARP ⅜-inch rocker arm studs, and a set of Manley Performance 2.02-inch intake and 1.60-inch stainless-steel exhaust valves.

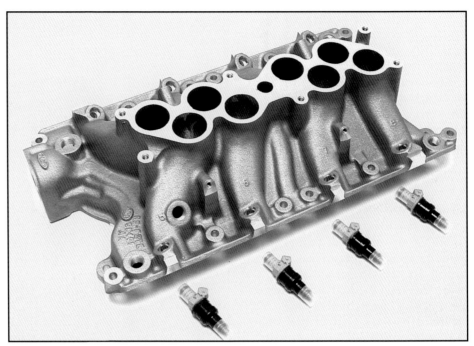

Our big-inch 408 Windsor's induction system consists of a FRT 351W GT40 lower intake and a set of MSD 60 lb/hr electronic fuel injectors.

Bolted to the top is an FRT Cobra M-9424-D52 cast-aluminum intake plenum, which ingests huge amounts of oxygen through a Ground Pounder Performance Products adjustable venture 65- to 75-mm billet-aluminum throttle body, which comes black anodized.

more room to play, so after about a half-hour cool down, Brule and Habrzyk conducted a third and final pull. Changes included increasing the timing to 22 degrees of advance and replacing the 100 octane with some 114-octane leaded fuel.

Max Engine Torque: 775.6 ft-lbs at 4,300 rpm

Max Horsepower: 753 hp at 5,400 rpm

We all realized that since the last pull was conducted using leaded racing fuel at 15.5 psi, you technically couldn't use this combination on the street. But on the racetrack, it's an entirely different story.

"This is a really good street engine," says Habrzyk. "Intake runner length obviously dictates low-end torque, and low-end torque on this engine is fabulous for the simple reason that with the GT40/Cobra intake, we have a lot of runner length. However, the problem with that is that the engine will not rev up to 7,000 rpm. Obviously, some of that has to do with the camshaft. And some of it has to do with the intake manifold. If you were to change out the upper intake plenum with something like a composite air box, or switch to a short runner EFI intake like the Edelbrock Victor Jr. throttle body intake manifold, it would kill some of the bottom-end torque, which with this engine you can sacri-

fice. After all, too much torque will simply blow off the tires. More importantly, by going to the air box, you would actually increase engine RPM and peak horsepower considerably, perhaps up to 40 to 50 hp, and that's what you're going to need."

How about the amount of boost produced by the Vortech V-7YSi-Trim Renegade supercharger?

"We were well above 12-lbs boost at higher RPM," says Tom. "One problem that we ran into at higher RPM is that with the single idler pulley setup, we experienced some blower belt slippage.

Installing a second idler tensioner pulley would obviously cure that!"

So there you have it – a 753-hp Vortech-supercharged 408 Windsor stroker for a price of around $10,000 to $12,000, minus engine builders and machine shop charges. This is a really great engine for any serious street racer, entry-level bracket racer, or Fun Ford Weekend Series True Street competitor to drop into a late-model Mustang, Thunderbird, or Cougar. Of course, with that much torque on tap, you're going to have to do a little chassis work to keep the darned thing from twisting up like a pretzel!

1. With an engine this big we need all the airflow we can get. Extrude Hone AFM technician Willie Melendez initially tested our intake to come up with a creditable baseline to work from.

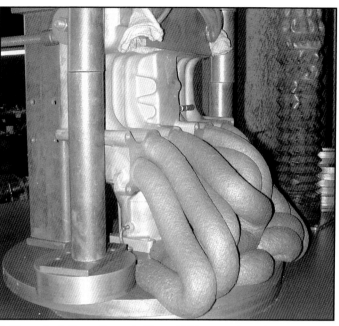

2. Then the folks at Extrude Hone AFM poured on the power putty. After completion, our combination GT40/Cobra intake showed an overall average flow increase of 39 percent.

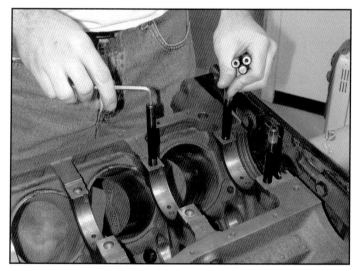

3. Block setup includes installing a set of ARP 154-5403 ½-inch screw-in main studs.

4. The next order of business is installing the set of Childs & Albert main bearings for the crank to ride on during initial mock-up.

5. The Probe Industries stroker crank is planted in place and the number one rod and piston assembly is installed. Adequate clearance is then checked.

6. *Our first problem area proves to be the rear lip on the crank. It rubs against the oil slinger lip recess area on the block. About 0.060 inch is machined off this area and everything is okay.*

7. *Another problem area is the number one crank throw which ever so slightly touches the oil pump mounting boss. Minor clearancing is required.*

8. *One of our Eagle 4340 forged-steel H-beam connecting rods and SRP forged-aluminum piston assemblies is mocked up using the provided dual spiro-locks that came with the pistons.*

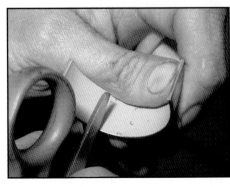

9. *After performing a 3-angle valve job on our FRT Z304 alloy heads, they are built using the Manley and Crane Cams valvetrain hardware. Note the 3-angle valve job and the close proximity of the valvesprings to the head stud bosses.*

10. *Prior to assembly, the rod bearings are chamfered to achieve ideal rod journal to rod bearing clearance. The bearings are then buffed with a Scotch-Brite pad to check for any high spots.*

11. Prior to installing the rod and piston assemblies, the top ring gap is checked and a measurement of 0.022-inch of piston ring gap clearance was achieved.

12. One of the final steps in preassembly is checking the bearing crush (inner and outer bearing-to-crank diameter). It registered a measurement of 3.002 inches on the main bearings, and a measurement of 2.999 inches on the main journals.

13. The rod bearings and rod journals are mic'ed out. A measurement of 2.1015 inches was achieved on the rod bearings, while a measurement of 2.0999 inches on the rod journals was recorded.

14. With bearing clearances properly checked, it's time to permanently install the Probe Industries 408-ci stroker crank.

15. The thrust bearing is installed, which was lapped in to achieve an optimum thrust bearing side-to-side clearance of 0.005 inch.

16. Our 408's ARP ½-inch main studs are torqued center out in increments of 80, 110, and finally 130 ft-lbs of torque.

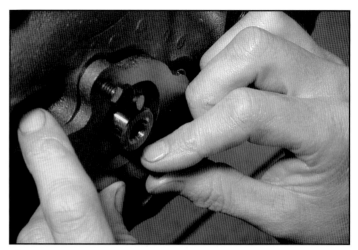

17. *Next comes installing the Crane Power Max roller cam and cam thrust plate using plenty of assembly lube. The cam is dialed in according to the information provided on the Crane Cam card, and then the ⅜-inch bolt on the cam thrust plate is final-torqued to 36 ft-lbs.*

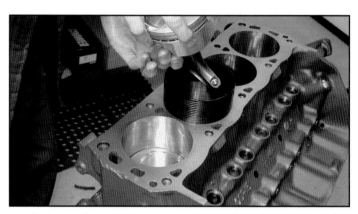

18. *At this point, our installer bolts up the Elgin-Cloyes Tru-Roller multiple index timing chain and torques the ⅜-inch timing chain bolt to 35 ft-lbs.*

19. *A piston ring compressor is used to install rod and piston assembly Number One, after which the main cap is installed. The ⁷⁄₁₆-inch ARP cap screw rod bolts are finger tightened. Then the remaining seven rod and piston assemblies are hung.*

20. *Our 408's ⁷⁄₁₆-inch ARP-equipped connecting rods are torqued starting from the center-out, torquing them to 70 ft-lbs using ARP's special moly "lube in a tube."*

21. *The next order of business is installing the ARP ½-inch screw-in head studs using a ⅜-inch Allen wrench to run them into the bosses.*

22. One of the final steps in preassembly is checking the bearing crush (inner and outer bearing-to-crank diameter). It registered a measurement of 3.002 inches on the main bearings, and a measurement of 2.999 inches on the main journals.

23. Prior to final-torquing the heads, our engine builder installs the Crane Cams roller lifters using plenty of assembly lube.

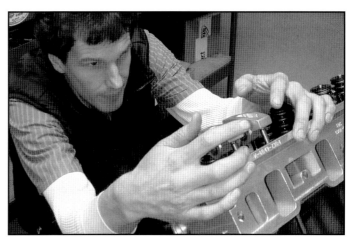

24. Our technician installs the ARP ⅜-inch rocker arm studs and FRT guide plates loosely on the Z304 head. This is done in order to ascertain that the guide plates align correctly with the 1.6:1 ratio Crane Cams roller rocker arms.

25. Satisfied with what he sees, our engine builder torques all rocker arm studs to 65 ft-lbs.

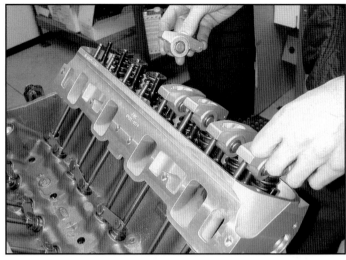

26. With rocker arm studs tightened, the next order of business is installing the Crane 8.100-inch pushrods. Then on go all 16 Crane roller rocker arms using the provided hardware.

27. The ARP head studs are torqued to 100 ft-lbs in increments of 75, 90, and 100 ft-lbs of torque.

28. After spreading on a generous bead of silicone-based gasket material across the ends of our 408's lifter valley, the Extrude Honed GT40 lower intake is installed using a series of ⅝₆-inch ARP stainless-steel cap screw bolts. These bolts are final-torqued to 30 ft-lbs, again working from the center-out. Then the sheetmetal valve covers are installed.

29. After test-fitting the FRT high-volume oil pump, we discover that the main support rib hits the front crank throw. ¹⁄₁₆ inch of material 1½ inches in length is ground in order to achieve proper clearance without compromising the structural integrity of the pump.

30. Heading into the home stretch, we see Central Coast Mustang's black anodized variable-venturi 65- to 75-mm throttle body being installed using a series of four ⁵⁄₁₆-inch bolts.

31. Fuel Air Spark Technology's stand-alone system for the Ford 351W is the company's basic bread- and -butter model. When used with a magnetic crank trigger system like an MSD 864, it can be used to control fuel, spark, and ignition, as well as other engine management functions.

32. One of the key power makers in this scenario is Vortech's Renegade V-7YSi-Trim gear charger, which is capable of producing 20 psi when equipped with a 3-inch Renegade cog belt drive pulley.

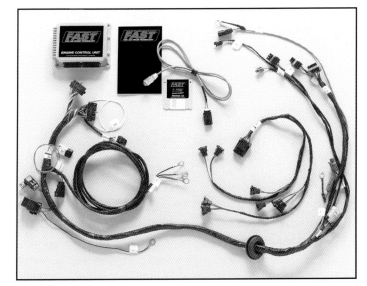

33. Shown is the processor and C-Com-WP Windows®-based software program disc that drives the F.A.S.T. engine management system.

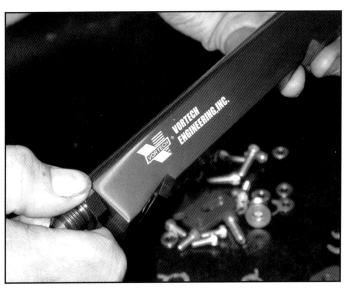

34. Vortech V-7YSi-trim supercharger installation begins with setting up our 408 Windsor stroker by installing the 6AN ¾-inch fuel line fittings into the ends of the Vortech fuel rails.

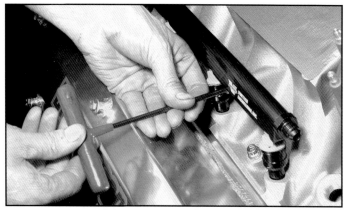

35. With all eight MSD 65 lb/hr High Flow fuel injectors installed into their ports, the Vortech fuel rails are installed onto the FRT GT40 lower intake using the provided brackets and 1/4-20 mounting bolts. Then injectors are permanently fixed in position using the provided spring-steel C-clips.

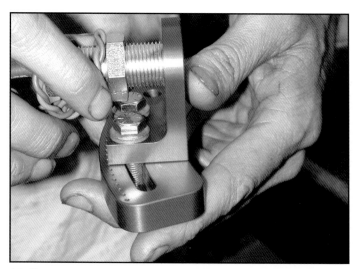

36. Here we see our installer setting up the MSD Flying Magnet Crank trigger pickup and mounting bracket.

37. The next step is to test-fit the MSD magnetic crank trigger wheel to the FRT stainless-steel harmonic engine balancer using the provided spacer.

38. After installing the crank trigger wheel in the correct rotation along with the Vortech V-7YSi-Trim lower crank pulley (which is secured to the damper via four ⅜-inch bolts), the crank trigger magnetic pickup mounting bracket is bolted to the passenger side of the timing chain cover using a pair of ⁵⁄₁₆-inch (18 x 3) bolts.

39. A difficult aspect of supercharger installation is the placement of the oil feed line fitting, which is located 1½ inches back and 1¾ inches down from the front sump directly below the front of the FRT oil pan drain bolt. A mark is made using a punch.

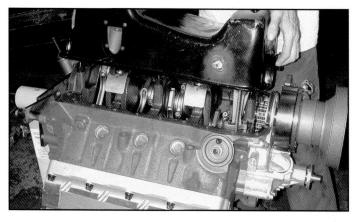

40. However, rather than using the suggested NPT pipe tap, the oil pan is removed and a clean ½-inch hole is drilled in the oil pan. The fitting is then welded on, and the oil pan is reinstalled onto our 408 using the combination-size ARP oil pan bolts. The beauty of setting up a supercharged engine outside the car is that you can do it right.

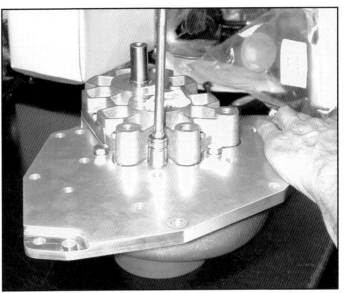

41. Since this engine has to be transported via truck to the Westech Performance Group's dyno shop, in essence we're just trial-fitting the Vortech Renegade system to make sure that everything fits correctly. The supercharger spacer plate and mounting bracket is installed to the drivers-side cylinder head using a single 3 x $\frac{7}{16}$-inch-long bolt to hold it in position.

42. The supercharger mounting plate is bolted to the supercharger using a series of three 1-inch bolts.

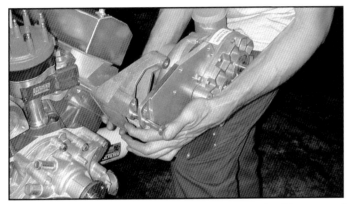

43. Using a pair of $\frac{7}{16}$ x 7½-inch-long bolts, the blower and mounting plate is installed to the V-7YSi-Trim supercharger mounting bracket.

44. This bracket is subsequently installed using the provided spacers and $\frac{3}{8}$ x 3-inch bolts.

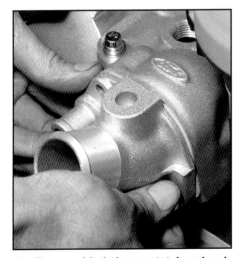

45. The provided thermostat housing is installed onto the front of the FRT GT40 intake using the provided gasket and bolts.

46. The alternator bracket is installed using two $\frac{3}{8}$ x 5½-inch bolts and one $\frac{7}{16}$ x 5½-inch bolt. We've taken our 408 as far as we can take it – until it goes to the dyno shop!

47. Once at the dyno shop, our 408 is filled up with 6 quarts of 10/30 Royal Purple Racing Oil prior to strapping this big brute onto the Westech's Super Flow 901 dyno.

48. A drill motor is used to run up the oil pressure. Our 408's "blood pressure" checks in at a very healthy 68 lbs.

49. Setting up the crank trigger ignition and distributor comes next. Using the F.A.S.T. Engine Management System in bank-to-bank mode, initial warm-up runs were conducted with Union 76 92-octane unleaded pump gas with the ignition set at 20-degrees advance.

51. Tom Habryzk and Westech Performance CEO John Baechtel prepare to install our 408 onto the dyno for the first time. Setup is understandably time consuming. All told, about 6 hours were required prior to getting our big-inch Ford to cackle.

50. Pre-dyno setup included building the air intake system using various lengths of 3½-inch, 90-degree aluminum tubing, joined together by neoprene hoses and hose clamps.

52. With 20-degrees advance in the ignition and Union 76 92-octane unleaded in the tank, our dyno tech very methodically breaks in our Vortech supercharged 408 stroker.

53. Initial pulls in unblown trim reveal a best of 455 hp at 4,700 rpm with 559.9 ft-lbs of torque at 3,500 rpm.

54. Satisfied with the initial dyno pull, the blower belt is hooked up, and then the ducting – it's time to rock 'n' roll!

55. The aspirated version of our 408 stroker roars to life. With 20-degrees advance in the ignition and 100-octane Rockett Brand unleaded race gas in the tank, our big, bad, blown Ford cranked out 707 hp at 5,300 rpm and 755.1 ft-lbs of torque at 4,300 rpm at 12.3 lbs boost!

56. With 114-octane leaded Rockett Brand race gas in the tank and 22-degrees advance in the distributor, our big-inch Windsor produced 15.5 lbs of boost, an incredible 753 hp at 5,400 rpm and 775.6 ft-lbs of torque at 4,300 rpm.

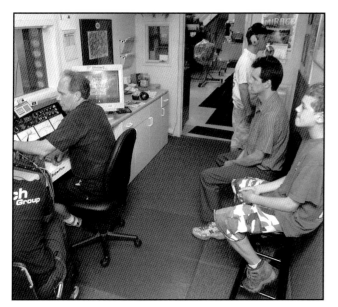

SOURCES

Central Coast Motorsports
426 North Curry Street
Tehachapi, CA 93561
Phone: (661) 823-2400
Fax: (661) 823-2407
Email: bigrdh@earthlink.com

Paul Williams Specialties
6732 Charity Avenue, Bay 7
Bakersfield, CA 93308
Phone: (661) 864-1632

Westech Performance Group
11098 Venture Drive, Unit "C"
Mira Loma, CA 91752
Phone: (951) 685-4767
www.westechperformance.com

PARADISE PAXTON TWIN SN-60 SUPERCHARGER INSTALLATION

When we looked at this setup, all we could think of was the old racer's adage, "If one is good, then two is better!" Of course, Craig Conley, the owner of Paradise Paxton, offered a more plausible explanation. He insisted that the Two-Stage and Straight Blow-Through twin supercharger kits were designed to deliver between 10 and 14 lbs of safe boost using the readily available pulley system on the engine.

This is nothing but good news for Ford enthusiasts who already have a Paxton supercharger setup on their car, as well as for those who are planning to install one in the very near future.

"Obviously, since you're going to be running a lot of boost, you need a healthy stock (8.5:1) compression engine to begin with. We highly recommend that you run a set of forged-aluminum pistons, and a blower cam with a lobe separation of between 110 and 112 degrees in order to maximize the blower's potential. We also recommend that you either O-ring the heads or run a high-grade material competition-style head gasket, along with a set of head studs."

Installing the two-stage Paxton twin supercharger setup is as simple as installing one of Paradise Paxton's beefy ⅜-inch thick, 6061 T-6-aluminum mounting plates, and SN-60-cased blowers. If you already have a Paxton SN-60 blower, you can use it with the twin kit, which also works with the factory 4-barrel carburetor and intake.

"We've made it possible to order either our two-stage or straight blow-through kits with either a pair of internally updated Paxton SN-60 blowers or with the polished SN-2000-type cases, and we also offer an optional polished or anodized billet-aluminum blower plate with either kit!"

Installing one of Paradise Paxton's straight blow-through twin supercharger systems on your vintage Shelby or

Shown is Paradise Paxton's Two-Stage Deluxe SN-60-based twin supercharger kit for 1964 1/2 to 1970, 260 ci to 302W-equipped Mustang and Shelby small-block Ford V-8 engines. This kit features two internally updated SN-60 Paxton superchargers, a heavy-duty ⅜-inch aluminum mounting plate, a cast-aluminum two-stage air box, an 8-rib serpentine crank pulley, a high volume mechanical fuel pump, K&N Lifetime conical air filter and air filter mounting bracket, and all the necessary hoses, supercharger mounting plate mounting studs, and bolts.

Mustang isn't any more complicated than installing the two-stage kit. However, if you don't already have one, you will need to pick up a factory Ford inline dual-quad intake, or a top-quality reproduction like a Blue Thunder, an Edelbrock, or Holley/Weiand, along with a pair of 600-cfm Holley carbs.

"We recommend a set of 600-cfm, vacuum-secondary Holley carburetors for street applications, or a set of 600- to 660-cfm Holley center squirters for race setups. That's one blower per carburetor! With the single-stage setup, we roughly estimate that you can double the amount of horsepower. And with the dual quad setup, we estimate an additional 10 to 15 percent gain."

"We designed both of these setups so that they would be minimal hassle to

install onto a stock 260-302 engine, although you will have to make a couple of minor modifications."

You'll have to relocate the battery to the trunk since you'll need that area to mount the air cleaner. With certain aftermarket water pumps, you may have to trim approximately 1 inch off the heater hose neck (don't worry, there's still plenty of material left) to accommodate one of the mounting studs. Other than that, everything else is strictly bolt-on!

Of course, seeing is believing, so follow along with us as Craig Conley and his crew at Paradise Paxton install one of their twin SN-60 straight blow through setups on this dual quad-equipped 1966 Mustang coupe.

Shown here is Paradise Paxton's straight blow-through design deluxe SN-60-based twin supercharger kit for 1964 1/4 to 1970, 260 ci to 302W-equipped Mustang and Shelby small-block Ford V-8 engines.

Shown is your average 8.5:1 compression dual-quad 289 Ford small-block engine. It is used to power Paradise Paxton's 1965 R&D mule, an SCCA Sedan racing replica.

1. The first order of business is removing the OE external mechanical fuel pump, which is replaced by Paradise Paxton's high volume mechanical fuel pump.

2. Next, the alternator is removed. The fan belt and fan are removed in order to install the Paradise Paxton 8-rib serpentine belt crank pulley onto the existing v-belt-drive pulley setup.

3. This is a simple procedure, and pulley mounting is accomplished by substituting the series of three OE ⅜-inch factory bolts with three ⅜-inch-long Allen-head bolts provided in the kit.

4. The coil is temporally unbolted and set aside. It is reinstalled to the new supercharger mounting plate with the coil-mounting bracket reversed.

5. A total of five 1 1/16-inch hex-head studs are installed, three of which are screwed on threaded mounting bosses on the right-side head.

6. Two more are installed, which are screwed into the threaded mounting bosses on the left-side head.

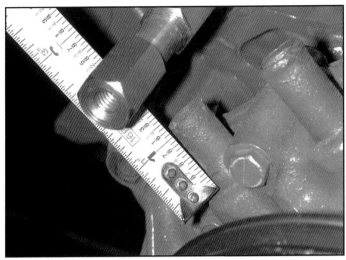

7. Prior to going any further, it may be necessary to trim approximately 1 inch of material off the heater hose nipple on the water pump. This is done to clear the inner stud and to provide enough clearance for the rubber hose. Don't worry; there is still enough material left.

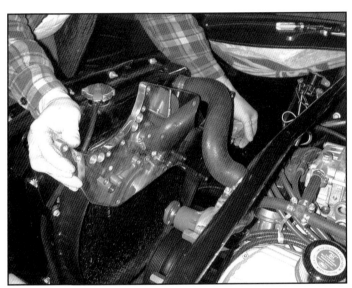

8. On goes the bracket, which is held in place by a series of six ⅜ x 16 grade-8 hex-head bolts and one ⅜ x 16 countersunk Allen-head bolt.

9. Since you want to be careful not to strip out the threads on the mounting bosses, a simple wrench or air ratchet is used to tighten things up.

10. Our alternator is remounted in position at the underside of the supercharger mounting bracket.

11. The supercharger idler pulley is mounted to the mounting plate using a ½-inch bolt.

12. Next the coil is repositioned and mounted to the backside of the supercharger mounting plate.

13. From there our installer bolts up the drivers-side SN-60 supercharger assembly using the supplied ⁵⁄₁₆-inch bolts that come with the kit.

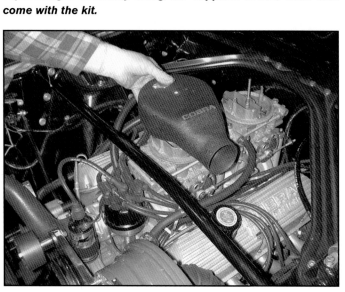

14. Next comes installing the drivers-side supercharger air intake duct and K&N conical air filter assembly.

15. This is followed with installing the forward blow-through bonnet and hose assembly.

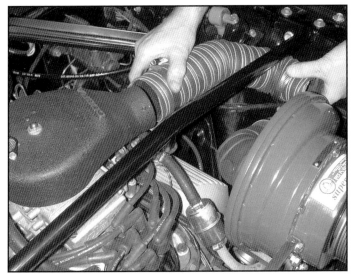

16. Next comes installing the passenger side Paxton SN-60. This unit is correctly clocked from the factory for proper engine clearance and to prevent any installation mistakes.

17. Rear air bonnet and air intake hose installation, reinstallation of the fan and accessory drive fan belt, and installation of the 8-rib serpentine blower drive belt come next.

18. Heading into the home stretch, the passenger side K&N conical air cleaner and air cleaner bracket are installed where the battery used to reside.

19. Installing the boost lines to both superchargers comes next.

20. And this is what the twin Paxton supercharged, straight blow-through dual-quad setup looks like completed. Now it's off to the dyno shop!

EATON/MAGNUSON SUPERCHARGERS

There is one supercharger that outnumbers all the others by a wide margin for a number of good reasons. Automotive giant Eaton Industries developed the Eaton supercharger, with the assistance of veteran supercharger legend Jerry Magnuson. Numerous incarnations of this small but amazingly efficient supercharger have appeared on a wide variety of factory installations, ranging from the 3.8L '89 Ford Thunderbird Super Coupe to the 4.6L 2003 and 2004 SVT Cobra. In fact, Eaton Industries supplies 98 percent of the domestic and international OE supercharger market, making them the largest supercharger manufacturer in the world!

Over the years, Magnuson has had a fruitful and continuing relationship with Eaton, and offers high-performance upgrades or variants based on Eaton supercharger products, which some people refer to as an "Eaton with an Attitude." As of this writing, Magnuson Products, Inc. is the only Eaton-authorized repair station, and Jerry works extremely hard to keep that distinction.

During the early 1980s, Eaton responded to a subtle industry call for a compact supercharger design that possessed extremely high volumetric efficiency, the ability to operate quietly, and the durability to outlive most of the engines it would be mounted on. Magnuson, who had manufactured his own

A number of Ford vehicles have come with Eaton superchargers direct from the factory. This one appeared on the Mach III concept car, which foreshadowed the supercharged '03 and '04 4.6-liter Cobras.

brand of supercharger (Magna-Charger) of ingenious, hybrid-rotor Roots-type superchargers for many years, was recruited to work with Eaton engineer Kris Berry, who was assigned to the task of reinventing the supercharger to meet OE demands.

The two eventually arrived at a design that looked somewhat similar to a Roots blower, but a closer look revealed

an entirely different animal. The most significant differences are that the Eaton's rotor speed is remarkably high, and its intake charge enters the unit and exits under pressure from one or the other of its flat faces (front or rear), which is the area you would expect the supercharger drive gears to be located. These various exits have been optimized for installations on vehicles like the second-

Ford's 1989 release of the 3.8L pushrod V-6 engine Thunderbird Super Coupe heralded the introduction of the compact, high-winding, Eaton supercharger. It was designed and developed by Eaton Corporation's Kris Berry, consultant Jerry Magnuson, and the Eaton design team. A total of $25 million was invested prior to ever bolting the first unit onto an engine. The Thunderbird Super Coupe was capable of producing a very creditable 210 hp and 315 ft-lbs of torque on unleaded pump gas.

generation Ford SVT Lightning pickup, 2003-04 SVT Mustang Cobra, and a variety of GM production vehicles.

According to Magnuson, one of the drawbacks to the Roots design can be found in a shift in VE as its drive speed increases with engine RPM. A typical Roots design can only muster a VE level of about 75 percent, unless it has been very carefully fine-tuned. That performance ceiling comes mostly because there just isn't time to fill the rotor voids. The air must travel quite a ways down between the rotor vanes, and the large rotors require case clearances that allow an unavoidable amount of leakage. This adds up to a VE that is livable, but not what Eaton was after.

Eaton needed a minimum of pumping losses, which can be reduced by more precise clearances. However, in the real world, exacting tolerances and the possibility of dirty air filters don't get along. The solution to this particular demand came in the form of better dynamic sealing through a novel rotor vane shape, mixed with some applied experience on the part of Berry and Magnuson.

The two engineers began with a clean sheet of paper, open minds, and enough Eaton engineering capital to do the job

This computer-generated art clearly shows the air path(s) generated by the Eaton supercharger. Intake air (A) becomes pressurized as it enters the supercharger. The air (B) then flows forward of the engine to the intercooler, returning to the intake manifold inlet at the rear of the engine (C). Bypass air (D) is then closed off to isolate the low-pressure air intake from the elevated pressure delivered from the supercharger.

Bypass Open: Intake air is drawn directly into the intake. Blower and intercooler are effectively out of the intake tract.

Bypass Closed: Intake air is drawn directly into the blower. No airflow is allowed through the electrically (solenoid) operated bypass valve, providing a pressure barrier. Air exits the blower and returns to the intake manifold through the factory ducting.

The introduction of the Mach III concept cars originally started out as a back burner project by Team Mustang. They wanted to create excitement over the up-and-coming fall 1993 release of the code name SN-95 1994 Ford Mustangs. Built on Fox Mustang platforms, these two cars featured aerodynamic bodywork. Power came in the form of a pair of Eaton-supercharged 4.6L DOHC Flex Fuel Ford mod motors burning 108-octane methanol and gasoline. Rated at 450 hp, the Mach IIIs were highly instrumental in the development of the Eaton-supercharged 4.6L DOHC SVT Mustang Cobra, which was released in 1996.

properly. Bringing the intake air charge into the unit at one end of a pair of computer-optimized smaller rotors offered many advantages over the Roots "down and around" airflow design. Most significantly, Eaton's new design allowed much longer rotor-port timing than was ever possible with the Roots design. Using a smaller case and rotor diameter meant tighter rotor-case sealing. Finally, the ability to turn the rotors at speeds that would cause a Roots to explode brought about some surprising advantages.

One of the most remarkable improvements turned out to be the unit's response to energy in the inlet waves near to and surrounding its inlet port. A careful look at the inlet and outlet port shapes on any version of the Eaton reveals shapes and profiles that are anything but accidental, and distinctly unfriendly to the manufacturing process. They are in a word – bizarre. Developed in part through computer modeling and refined through thousands of hours of flow-bench time, the appearance of the ports is totally alien to anything that has appeared on a Roots before. This shape appears in a more extreme manner on the heavily modified units that come from Magnuson's West Coast "pump works."

To put it bluntly, these units like to be turned at ridiculous RPM, and they come back at you with a wall of energy. At a rotor speed of 5,000 rpm, the VE is in the neighborhood of 85 percent. At 10,000 rpm, the VE rises to about 89 percent. And at 15,500 rpm, the VE is close to 97 percent! In the interest of long-term reliability, the OEMs use pulley size to regulate a maximum operational limit of about 12,000 rpm. Jerry feels that his Eaton/Magnuson units are good for at least 15,000 rpm, and he isn't usually wrong about these kinds of things!

The high VE numbers mean you'll waste very little power trying to turn the supercharger into its sweet spot. This is the major difference from other, earlier supercharger designs. A very high pumping efficiency also results in cooler air, because the air isn't lingering around the rotors. This turns out to be a critical improvement in performance potential.

Surprising as it may seem, running these units at such an elevated RPM does not make them any noisier. The rotor vane shapes (modified involutes), the extremely precise balancing and manufacturing processes, and the unusual intake and exit port shapes allow the Eaton to operate without making much more noise than the normal accessories on a modern vehicle.

Every OEM installation of this design has incorporated a bypass valve located in the intake ducting. This valve is positioned at the inlet of the supercharger, and is operated by a combination of Electronic Control Module (ECM) and manifold pressure actuators in almost every instance. The purpose of this valve is to lighten the engine load under cruise conditions and allow a clean mode-switch as the driver stomps on the throttle. Under cruise conditions, the valve is open, allowing the intake manifold to receive inlet air without any involvement of the supercharger or intercooler (if there's an intercooler). As the engine demand calls for boost, the bypass valve closes, diverting intake air through the supercharger and into the intake manifold. This means that under cruise conditions, the supercharger is just freewheeling, without any significant power drain on the engine. With its small rotors, the unit doesn't make large demands on an engine in any case, but every little bit helps.

Eaton and Magnuson use the same general airflow-based scheme to identify their products. These callouts are usually 60, 90, or 120, referring to their ability to pump a certain volume of air in a single rotor revolution. Magnuson typically recommends his Ford Model 90 for small-block Ford engines displacing 351 ci or less. For much smaller engines (Ford's 260 and 289), Magnuson leans toward the Model 60 for street applications. In many instances, Jerry will make recommendations leaning more toward a more basic unit, either unaltered or with only slight internal modifications. He explains that although this may seem paradoxically wrong, a smaller unit – turned very fast, indeed – will provide incredible throttle response, and will keep up with any mildly-modified

The Ford-Eaton alliance continued with the 1998 introduction of the Ford F-150-based second-generation SVT Lightning sport trucks. A 5.4L 8.4:1 compression Triton modular engine V-8, using an intercooled Eaton Gen IV supercharger, powered the new Lightnings. They were capable of producing 360 hp at 5,250 rpm and 440 ft-lbs of torque at 3,000 rpm. With that much power on tap, the SVT Lightning was capable of reeling off 0 to 60 in 6.2 seconds, and full quarters in 14.6 seconds at 97 mph, making it the fastest (140 mph top end) and quickest sport truck on the planet.

GEORGE FABRY'S EATON-SUPERCHARGED

When was the last time you saw a supercharged, intercooled 3.8L Thunderbird Super Coupe engine transplanted into a 1940 Ford Deluxe sedan? George Fabry, a member of the Sabers car club of Denver, is rightfully proud of his rather unique machine.

"We pulled the engine out of an '89 Thunderbird Super Coupe. It's basically stock but with 210 hp on board, it runs really great!"

With a supercharger, intercooler, and all that factory ducting, it's a very

tight fit. In fact, Fabry had to turn the intercooler sideways to get it to fit under the hood. And what about those touchy engine management electronics?

"Fellow club member and Ford specialist Don Seyfer (Seyfer Automotive) adapted the Super Coupe engine wiring harness to the car and it works just great!"

Credit for the '40s outstanding paint and bodywork goes to George, who sprayed the sedan in PPG Raven Black. But how does Fabry's one-of-a-

kind '40 Deluxe two-door sedan perform?

"It runs down the road without a hitch. We've made quite a few lengthy road trips with the car (the Street Rod Nationals events at both Louisville and Oklahoma City, as well as trips to Spokane, Washington, and Yellowstone National Park) with zero problems. The thing just motors along down the highway at 70+ mph with the air conditioning (a combination Super Coupe and Vintique A/C system) running at full blast!"

3.8L '40 Ford

The fall 2002 release of the Eaton-supercharged SVT Mustang Cobra really rocked consumers with the Gen V Eaton–supercharged and intercooled 4.6L DOHC modular V-8. This rocket ship was capable of producing 390 hp and 390 ft-lbs of torque, although most seasoned auto writers felt that Ford was being VERY conservative about the horsepower figures.

this case, the rotor timing and inlet port of the supercharger) will slightly compress at its leading end. This creates a wave, or pulse, that travels back toward the initial source of the air. When the valve (or port) reopens, a negative wave is created in the tube (slight vacuum), and the air begins to flow through the valve again.

The intensity, speed, and frequency of those waves are determined primarily by the volume of the tube, the valve-open/closed frequency, the volume of air ingested for each valve cycle, and the valve area. In a tunnel-ram intake, the idea is to optimize these factors by changing the manifold's runner volume and length to suit what the carburetors need to stay under control, and to hopefully have a nice, firm pressure wave heading toward each intake valve when the time is right for it to open again.

With the insanely high rotor speed of the Eaton design, the wave timing is actually based more upon a harmonic of the actual valve-open frequency, but the effect is the same. A harmonic is a little like a playing card fanning against bicycle spokes instead of slapping the tire once per revolution. It is related to a recurring fundamental frequency, but typically in smaller increments that are equal divisions of that fundamental frequency.

The inlet of the Eaton supercharger is located relatively far from the intake manifold that, allowing for the generally springy nature of air, makes a nice, hard wave coming back from the valves difficult to use. However, there is enough of a wave available from the engine to exploit it around the inlet of the blower. This is one of the considerations you should make in deciding whether to go for the stock Eaton supercharger model or one of Jerry Magnuson's breathed-on Eaton/ Magnuson high-performance units. Both superchargers will turn at about the same RPM, they're both ridiculously efficient, and neither is noisy. A Magnuson-modified Eaton unit is optimized toward a more specific operating range in terms of engine RPM than is the unmodified Eaton.

Either unit is designed to operate over a wide range of RPM, of course, but if you were to drive the same Mustang,

small-block. With a more modified engine, especially if the cylinder heads have been seriously ported, Magnuson recommends his Model S-90, which is a worked-over Fifth-Generation Eaton.

As mentioned earlier, these superchargers take advantage of the inlet tract wave energy to almost completely (up to 97 percent) fill the voids between the rotor vanes. This effect is nearly identical to what happens in a properly designed tunnel-ram intake manifold with carburetors. Air is obviously a compressible medium. As such, a column of air pulled into a tube, then suddenly halted by a valve of any kind (in

Supercharger maven Jerry Magnuson is considered to be one of the leading authorities in the world on high-performance supercharger systems. Magnuson and his Ventura, California-based company, Magnuson Products Inc., were highly instrumental in the design and development of the Roots-type Eaton supercharger and related supercharger systems for OE applications like the 1989 Thunderbird Super Coupe, second-generation 1998 Ford Lightning, etc. Not only is Magnuson Products the official warranty repair and service depot for Eaton, but the company also offers numerous hybrid variations based on the Eaton design for Ford, GM, and Daimler-Chrysler applications.

Magnuson Products Inc. is world renown for building what many refer to as "an Eaton with an attitude." In this photo, a Magnuson technician is photographed running a volt check on either a Gen IV or Gen V Eaton/Magnuson bypass actuator solenoid to ensure that the unit is fail-safe.

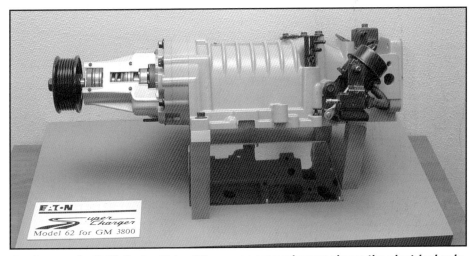

A cutaway of a 3800 Series Eaton/Magnuson supercharger shows the electrical solenoid-activated bypass actuator, which is used to "burp" the supercharger in-between gear changes. This is done so that it takes some of the power pit of the car's transmission to soften up the shifting.

for example, while conducting an A-B comparison of the two superchargers, you'll see a softer power curve over a slightly wider RPM range with the basic Eaton. The Magnuson-modified unit provides more intense power and a higher peak output. In most cases, that difference is hard to describe with a word like "dramatic"; perhaps incredible might be a better choice!

The Eaton and Ford Alliance

Ford was one of the first (if not the first) domestic automobile manufacturers to incorporate an Eaton supercharger on a production model. The Eaton-supercharged and intercooled 3.8L V-6 Thunderbird Super Coupe appeared in 1989, with a very creditable 210 hp and 315 ft/lbs of torque.

"When Ford first started talking about installing a 3.8L supercharged engine in these vehicles, Jerry (Magnuson) was recruited by Eaton Corporation as a consultant," said Magnuson Products Sales Manager Bob Roese.

"Rumor has it that before the Eaton engineering team ever bolted a supercharger onto a 3.8L Ford pushrod V-6 engine, they had over 25,000,000 dollars worth of development money invested in the project. Because of the federally mandated emissions rules and regulations, Ford required that this supercharger had to require zero maintenance!"

DE-RANGED RANGER

Conceived by Ford Special Vehicle Engineering (SVE) Powertrain Development engineer Dave Dempster and his staff, the 380-hp, 13-second Lightning Bolt concept show truck is one of the most exciting light-duty performance street truck projects to come along in a long, long time.

"The SVE Lightning Bolt was an idea that came to mind sometime in early 2002," says Dave Dempster with a smile. "It was kind of a backburner kind of a project. We had already built a supercharged 5.0L Ranger a few years back, and that project went over quite well. Since we had plenty of 5.4L SOHC power trains laying around from our second-generation Lightning R&D program, SVE engineers Keith Healy, Paul Gordineer, Dave Benhke, Scott Tate, and I just thought that it would really be a cool idea to try and shoehorn one of these Eaton-supercharged and intercooled power trains into one of these little trucks."

Of course, certain engineering criteria were set. One of the team's primary objectives was to preserve the prototype nature of the beast – in other words, use as many off-the-shelf parts as they could.

For example, with the exception of a K&N filtercharger system, a set of stainless-steel four-tube headers, and 3-inch Borla Super Pro mufflers, the engine powering this beast is 100 percent stock. And so is the stock-calibrated 700R4 transmission behind it. The remainder of the build is strictly custom.

With the Lightning power train set back in the Ranger chassis 2.5 inches and lowered 2 inches, it required a little creative engineering.

"We started with a 4-cylinder-powered 2002 Ranger pickup pulled straight off the assembly line. Knowing the torque that the supercharged 5.4L engine produces (450 ft-lbs), we knew that the stock chassis would never survive that kind of punishment, so we

boxed them (the frame rails) in to give them more strength."

The next order of business was setting up the truck's suspension. Out back you'll find a narrowed (9.75 inches) 9.8-inch Lightning rear axle assembly with 2.73:1 gears. The rear end is mounted to a set of Ranger dual-leaf rear springs dampened by Bilstein gas-charged shocks.

Up front you'll find a pair of Ford Lightning lower control arms, and Light-

ning front spindles, again with Bilstein gas-charged shocks. Steering gear on the truck was also upgraded to the Lightning power-assist, reciprocating-ball setup. Stopping is handled by a pair of 12-inch vented-rotor SVT Lightning disc brakes front and rear. The wheels are also off-the-shelf 18 x 9-inch SVT Lightning wheels, although the Michelin Pilot-equipped rear wheels have been slightly widened a total of 5 inches.

In order to accommodate the rather sizeable 5.4L Eaton-supercharged Lightning power train, Dempster and company had to do some creative packaging in the Ranger engine compartment.

"We had to modify the interior bulkhead (firewall) and move it back a total of 2.5 inches. In the process, we also had to fabricate a new transmission tunnel."

The Lightning Bolt team also had to remove the OE Ranger air conditioning unit and replace it with a more compact Ford Econoline rear control unit, which fits quite nicely. With creature comforts like Sof-Trim Manufacturing-covered OE black leather Ranger seats, Breed Technologies billet trim components, and a 450-watt Pioneer audio system, this Ranger provides comfort with performance.

The body and Ford Sonic Blue paint were handled by Ford body man Brian Shell. Weighing in at just 3,800 pounds, the Lightning Bolt concept truck has recorded a best of 13.6-seconds at 108 mph in the standing quarter, and since we've driven it, you can take our word for it when we tell you that it's fast as heck.

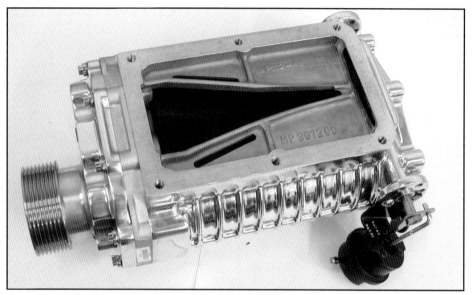

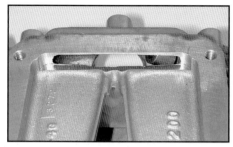

This view clearly shows the bypass ducting in the backside of the intake tract on the Eaton/Magnuson M112.

Shown is a polished version of the Eaton/Magnuson M112 unit, which would be used on a 4.6L SOHC Mustang, 4.6L DOHC Mustang Cobra, Ford SVT Lightning, or Harley Hauler Limited Edition Ford pickups.

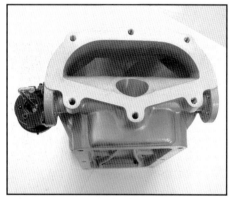

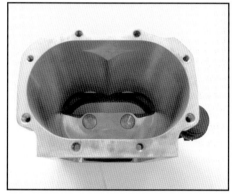

The Eaton/Magnuson supercharger housing is manufactured in-house at Magnuson Products. Note the finish on the inside of the case. The machining on these cases is VERY proprietary, and Magnuson is one of two facilities in the United States licensed by Eaton to do the job.

This shot clearly show the back of the Eaton/Magnuson M112 blower case. Note the Eaton rotor pack along with the electrical solenoid-activated bypass valve. Also note that this unit is internally coated with an abradable powder coating (APC), which zero clearances when run to increase the overall volumetric efficiency of the unit.

This view clearly shows the intake ducting on the bottom of the Eaton/Magnuson M112 supercharger. Certain changes have been made on the Magnuson units to enhance performance. For example, seal timing is changed on the bottom of the supercharger to increase the efficiency of the unit. And those long, narrow slots you see on the bottom side of the unit were put there to reduce the noise of the unit. This is so you don't hear the "pounding" air being inducted into the intake manifold.

Although they weren't production vehicles, Eaton/Magnuson superchargers made an appearance on the 4.6L DOHC Mach III Mustang show cars (there were two) built in 1992. Not officially recognized as legitimate concept cars by some of the hierarchy at Ford, the Mach III concept cars were really a backburner inter-department engineering exercise conducted by Team Mustang, then spearheaded by Will Bodie and O. J. "John" Coletti. These vehicles

were specifically intended to whet the whistle of new-car-starved Mustang enthusiasts worldwide before the long-awaited introduction of the exciting new SN-95 1994 Ford Mustangs.

The Lincoln Mk VIII-derived 4.6L DOHC engines that powered the Mach III Mustangs would ultimately be used in

the SVT Mustang Cobra production models, with a considerably more refined Eaton-supercharged version actually making an appearance in the 2003 SVT Mustang Cobra. However, the Mach III engines, rated at 450 hp, featured flex-fuel, clean air-engine packages, a feature the SVT Cobra wouldn't have. This allowed them to burn 108-octane M-85 fuel, which is a mix of 85 percent ethanol and 15 percent premium gasoline.

The Ford-Eaton alliance moved forward in 1995 with the introduction of the second-generation SVT Lightning pickup. Powered by a 5.4L Triton V-8 with 8.4:1 compression, the Gen II Lightning featured an Eaton Gen-IV supercharger with water-to-water intercooler. This package produced a whopping 440 ft-lbs of torque and 360 hp, and was capable of propelling the Lightning from 0 to 60 mph in 6.2 seconds, and earning quarter-mile times of 14.6 sec-

Shown is the Eaton-manufactured three-lobe, 60-degree, helix rotor pack developed by Eaton and Magnuson. It is the heart and soul of the Eaton/Magnuson supercharger product lines. Eaton exclusively manufactures these packs at its Athens, Georgia, facility.

Magnuson's blower dyno room stays plenty busy running and dyno-testing both Eaton rebuilds and brand-new Eaton/Magnuson units.

onds at 97 mph. With a top speed of 140 mph, the Lightning quickly became the fastest production pickup in the world.

Next up was the aforementioned Eaton supercharged and intercooled 4.6L DOHC 2003 SVT Mustang Cobra. Considered to the epitome of late-model Mustang performance, the SVT Mustang Cobra knocked out 390 hp and 390 ft-lbs of torque – although many who've driven the car swear it's more like 425 hp.

Magnuson Products, Inc.
1990 Knoll Drive
Ventura, CA, 93003
Phone: (805) 289-0044
Fax: (805) 677-4897
www.magnacharger.com
www.magnusonproducts.com

Private Label Eaton/ Magnuson Supercharger Systems

Allen Engine Development is located in the heart of supercharger country, just a stone's throw away from industry giants like Vortech, Paxton, and Magnuson. Eaton supercharger buffs will be happy to learn that Allen Engineering offers a total of nine (9) air-to-water intercooled supercharger packages for

Shown here is Allen Engine Development's Eaton Gen III M90s-based air-to-water intercooled supercharger kit for the 4.6L modular engine 1996-2003 Mustang GT, 4.6L engine "Bullitt" (with certain changes), and 4.6L 1996-1997 Ford Thunderbird. Test data reveals a horsepower increase of 100+ and 90 ft-lbs. Depending on which Mustang you have, 0 to 60 times run between 4.8 and 5.2 seconds, while quarter-mile clockings come in between 13.3 and 13.8 seconds at 102 to 108 mph!

Ford's 4.6L and 5.4L SOHC and DOHC modular V-8 engines for Mustang, Thunderbird, Crown Victoria/Grand Marquis, Explorer/Mountaineer, and F-150/F-250/Expedition models. These kits are all CARB certified and 50-state legal.

All of Allen Engine Development's modular engine supercharger systems feature the Eaton/Magnuson third-generation M90s supercharger as the centerpiece. They also come complete with a cast-aluminum supercharger intake manifold, an air-to-water intercooler, mechanical water pump, billet-aluminum fuel rails, supplemental fuel system regulator, electrically activated supercharger bypass valve, and all the necessary brackets, belts, hoses, and hardware to complete an OEM-quality installation.

Allen Engine Development thoroughly dyno tests all their Eaton/Magnuson Ford kits on Super Flow engine dynos using the Digi-log Data Acquisition System to achieve 100 percent accurate test data. So when you buy one of Allen's street supercharger kits, you know you're getting the real deal.

Allen Engine Development, Inc.
2521 Palm Drive
Ventura, CA 93003
Phone: (805) 658-8262
Fax: (805) 658-8645
www.allenengine.com

Ford Racing Performance Parts
44050 Groesbeck Highway
Clinton Township, MI 48036-1108
Phone: (810) 468-1356
www.fordracingparts.com

Saleen, Inc.
76 Fairbanks
Irvine, CA 92618
Phone: (800) 888-8945
www.saleen.com

Roush Performance Products
28156 Plymouth Road, Suite Z
Livonia, MI 48150
Phone: 1-800-59 ROUSH
Local: (734) 466-6222
Fax: (734) 466-6940
www.roushperf.com

Allen Engine Development Kit Applications

1996-1998 4.6L SOHC Mustang GT Rev-II kit, 100+ hp/90 ft-lb increase
1999-2002 4.6L Mustang GT, available in either 6 or 9 psi, 70-107+ hp/60-100 ft-lb increase
2001 4.6L Bullitt kit, available in either 6 or 9 psi, 70-107+ hp/60-100 ft-lb increase
1994-1997 4.6L Thunderbird, 97+ hp/74 ft-lb increase
1996-2002 Crown Victoria/Grand Marquis, 90 hp/80 ft-lb increase
4.6L Explorer/Mountaineer Rev II kit
1997-2002 4.6L F-150/Expedition kit
1997-2002 5.4L F-150/Expedition kit
2003 4.6L & 5.4L Expedition kit

Allen Engine Development manufactures its own air-to-water intercoolers for its kits.

The heart and soul of the Allen Engine Development kits is the Gen III Eaton/Magnuson M90s supercharger. Boost levels run from 6 to 9 psi, depending on which kit you order.

Jack Roush and the boys at Roush Performance Products have also come up with their own Eaton/Magnuson-based supercharger kit for the 2001-2004 4.6L SOHC 2-valve modular engine Mustang, which bumps the horsepower up some 40+. However, the folks at Roush are very quick to point out the fact that the kit is far from a simple bolt-on blower kit. Over 150 parts are included. The list includes (among other things) an electronic fuel pump and tank, alternator, flywheel, intake manifolds, front engine accessory drive (FEAD), and power train control module (PCM). To date, over 50 Roush vehicles have been sold with the Eaton/Magnuson-based Roush supercharger installed. This kit can be ordered through any Roush dealer, or through the www.roushparts.com website.

TWIN-SCREW BLOWERS

Because of its ability to produce an abundance of boost at virtually any engine RPM without any supercharger lag, the twin-screw compressor has become one of the most popular choices for contemporary street supercharging. Former NHRA Top Fuel and Funny Car racer Art Whipple was highly instrumental in introducing twin-screw compressor technology to the world of drag racing. He also went on to popularize the concept with the automotive performance aftermarket by developing a complete series of GM-derived, Lysholm-based Whipple twin-screw supercharger kits.

Simultaneously, Jim Bell (Kenne Bell, Inc.), long known as the builder of some of the fastest and quickest Buick Grand National cars in the country, began experimenting with the Autorotor-derived twin-screw compressor. The by-product of that grand experiment was the 1.5L Kenne-Bell TS-1500 twin-screw supercharger kit for the 1986 and up 5.0L pushrod V-8 engine Mustangs. But how does the twin-screw compressor design really work?

"The basic engineering philosophy behind the creation of the twin-screw compressor is that the shortest, smoothest path between two points is always best for optimum airflow," commented Jim Bell.

Bell went on to explain that depending on the application, as air enters through the rear or top rear of a Kenne Bell twin-screw supercharger case, the "male" rotor rotates clockwise while the

Kenne Bell offers a number of twin-screw supercharger kits, including kits to upgrade your factory supercharged Cobra and Lightning, and kits to supercharge your naturally aspirated Mustang or truck.

"female" rotor rotates counterclockwise to internally compress the air producing a much higher VE. This is opposite of the operating principles of a Roots design, which is considered to be a semi-blow-through design.

"This was done to avoid pumping air between the rotors and case," says Bell. "This more efficient method of internal compression also reduces the high turbulence, friction, and heat buildup (known as adiabatic efficien-

cy) inside the case during the process of trapping and compressing the air between the rotors, ultimately producing a lower air-charge temperature. The significantly compressed and cooler air charge is then screwed, or propelled, toward the front of the case, where it's discharged into the engine."

Due to its superior design, the twin-screw compressor also requires (depending on the size of the supercharger drive

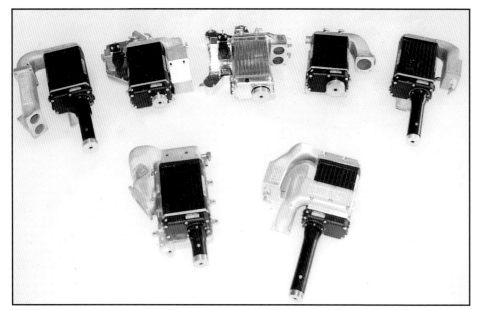

Kenne Bell Superchargers offers a full line of Autorotor-based twin-screw superchargers for Ford, DaimlerChrysler, and GM applications ranging from the 0.87L, 1.33L, 1.5L, 1.7L, 1.8L, 2.0L, 2.2l, 2.4L, and 2.6L dimensions.

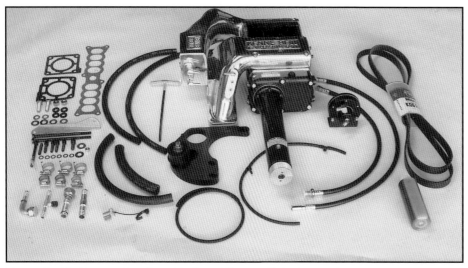

Kenne Bell's 50-state-legal 1.5L bolt-on TS-1500 Twin-Screw Supercharger Kit for the 1986-1995 5.0L pushrod V-8 engine Mustangs delivers 6 to 8 psi.

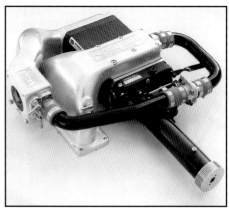

Shown is Kenne Bell's 1986-1995 2.2L Blowzilla supercharger upgrade for the 5.0L Ford pushrod V-8 engines with bypass valve, 6 to 12 psi.

pulley) 10 to 16 less horsepower to drive, a noteworthy reduction in parasitic loss. Of course, the end result is increased horsepower and torque at any operating speed, which equates to increased acceleration for quick starts, straight-line running, passing, towing, or hill climbing. "It's like having a big-block under the hood," says Jim Bell with a huge grin.

Although Kenne Bell offers a total of nine different sizes of self-cooled, self-lubricating twin-screw superchargers, there currently are three different sizes used in their Ford-specific kits. Each of the Autorotor-based Kenne Bell street superchargers is 50-state legal.

There's the billet-aluminum-cased 1.5L TS-1500, which is capable of producing a 40 percent gain in rear wheel horsepower at boost levels of up to 12 psi max boost. There's the slightly larger 1.7L billet-aluminum-cased TS-1700 interim compressor, which is capable of producing between 45 and 50 percent more horsepower to the rear wheels in normal trim, and up to 55 to 60 percent more horsepower when intercooled at 13 psi. Then there's the even larger 2.2L billet-aluminum-cased TS-2200, which Bell and company affectionately refer to as the Blowzilla 2200, capable of producing 70 to 75 percent more rear wheel horsepower at 18 psi max boost!

All three units occupy virtually the same physical space inside the engine compartment of any model 1986 to 1995 5.0L Mustang or Ford F-150, or 1996 to 2004 4.6L SOHC Mustang GT or DOHC SVT Mustang Cobra. Listed below are the specific Kenne Bell Ford applications.

Kenne Bell 1986-1995 5.0L Mustang LX, GT, and Cobra, 1.5L, TS-1500 Twin-Screw Supercharger Kit available in satin, black, or optional polished, rated at 450 hp

Kenne Bell 1986-1995 5.0L Mustang LX, GT, 2.2L, Blowzilla TS-2200 Twin-Screw Supercharger Upgrade Kit, available in satin, black, or optional polished, rated at 675 hp

Kenne Bell 1994-1995 5.8L F-150/SVT Lightning F-150 pickup, 1.5L, TS-1500 Twin-Screw Supercharger Kit, available in satin, black, or optional polished

Kenne-Bell 1994-1995 5.8L Ford F-150/SVT Lightning F-150 pickup, 2.2L, Blowzilla 2200 Supercharger Upgrade Kit, available in satin, black, or optional polished

Kenne Bell 1998-2001 5.4L SVT Lightning, 2.0L, 96+ hp Supercharger Upgrade, available in satin, black, or optional polished

Kenne Bell 1996-2004 4.6L Mustang GT, 1.5L, TS-1500 Twin-Screw Super-

Kenne Bell's 2.2L Blowzilla twin-screw supercharger has been successfully used on all 1996-2003 4.6L DOHC SVT Mustang Cobra models. The company has recently prototyped a system for the 4.6L DOHC engine Mach 1 cars, at 20 psi max boost. Shown here is a fully installed 2.2L twin-screw Mach 1 system showing not only the blower, but also the (prototype) shaker hood scoop brackets, which are an integral part of the Kenne Bell kit.

charger Kit, available in satin, black, or optional polished, optional intercooler

Kenne Bell 1996-2004 4.6L Mustang GT, 2.2L, Blowzilla TS-2200 Twin-Screw Supercharger Upgrade Kit, available in satin, black, or optional polished, optional intercooler

Kenne Bell 1996-2004 4.6L DOHC SVT Mustang Cobra, 2.2L, Blowzilla TS-2200 Twin-Screw Supercharger Kit, 9 psi, available in satin, black, or optional polished, optional intercooler

These 100 percent bolt-on Kenne Bell supercharger kits look so factory it's kind of hard to tell that they're actually aftermarket. Furthermore, K.B. states that their twin-screw supercharger kits are the only kits on the market that allow all the OEM engine accessories to remain in the stock position.

Kenne Bell is also working on a 1.7L, 50-state-legal twin-screw supercharger kit (10 psi max boost) for the 4.6L, 3-valve 2005 Mustangs. "A stock 2005 3-valve Mustang GT is capable of producing around 279 hp at the rear wheels," says Bell. "With our intercooled 1.7L-equipped R&D mule, we're currently able to produce 460 horsepower!"

More good news! Kenne Bell also offers a fourth model, the 2.4L Blowzilla 2400, which is capable of operating at an incredible 26 psi max boost. However, the 2.4L Blowzilla is for competition or "off road use only."

Of course, no matter what the application, actual boost, torque, and horsepower are relative to how quick you turn the compressor, and that is governed by the size of supercharger drive pulley you use.

"A general rule of thumb is that for each $\frac{1}{8}$ inch in diameter, you will produce 1-horsepower while simultaneously increasing PSI accordingly. Remember, a supercharger is a pump. As it tries to pump air into an engine, it (by sheer design) pumps more air than the engine can normally exhaust – the bigger the (cubic-inch displacement of an) engine the smaller the pulley. Depending on the actual application and size of the Kenne Bell Twin-Screw Supercharger being used, we offer over 40 different-sized drive pulleys for Ford small-blocks and

PoppTop Mustang

"There's no better sound than the high-winding pitch you get from a Kenne Bell supercharged 5.0L engine," says computer programmer and systems support specialist Kevin Popp, and we couldn't agree more.

"When I was 16 years old, I bought a '67 Mustang from a co-worker for $700," says Popp. "The car was so beat up I had to purchase a 6-cylinder Mustang donor car just so that I could salvage the whole deal. The more I worked on the car, the more I learned about Mustangs through swapping out the engine and transmission, the differential, the brakes, and everything else that was

required to bring this tired old pony back to life!"

In order to make his dream car project a reality, Popp took mechanic's classes at Denver's Vo-Tech University, and he's been involved with Mustangs ever since. However, one of the things that Kevin really learned to appreciate at school was the fine art behind the intricate workings of the electronically controlled 5.0L Ford small-block engine.

Not exactly being flush with cash, Popp bided his time until the day when he learned that the local Toyota dealer had taken a 1995 Sapphire Blue (that's purple) Mustang GT convertible in on trade.

"I told them that purple was not my favorite color, and that I was looking for a yellow GT instead. But I promised the salesman that I would at least come down and look at the car. And when I saw her I instantly fell in love!"

Popp immediately began researching factory data about his new toy. "I've been told that there are only 172 of these models produced with the white leather interior and white top," says Popp.

Wheels would be the first modification on Kevin's list. "I settled on a set of Cragar SS 980, 18-inch-five-spoke wheels, which really woke up the car."

Popp debuted his Mustang at the 1998 Rocky Mountain Mustang Roundup in Steamboat Springs, Colorado, and after checking out the competition, he came home with a ton of ideas. "I had originally intended to turn this car into a long-term project for me and my wife to do on weekends, but then on April 24 along came my son Conner just seven weeks before the 2004 Rocky Mountain Roundup. I decided that it might not be as easy to complete all the modifications I had planned with a new baby in the house, unless I completed them right away."

Parts began arriving at Popp's home on a regular basis, and the work began in earnest. "Being new parents, I got little sleep in-between working on the car, and adjusting to fatherhood! Thanks to an understanding wife and new mother, I was able to complete the project complete with a new Kenne Bell TS-1500 supercharger installed.

"The test drive back from the body shop was about all the fun Joyce got to have. I had wanted to add some ghost flames so that people would do a double-take whenever I drove by," says Popp. "The painter at UNI/TEC Auto Body and I discussed a few ideas and we came up with these three-dimensional chameleon ghost flames with orange highlights. Along the way, we also added a combination Saleen and ABC Exclusives body kit and tonneau cover. In the bright sun the car looks amazing."

While they were at it, the Popps also upgraded the GT's factory white leather interior with a combination of Saleen and AutoMeter white-face gauges, a Kenwood D-Mask six-disc CD changer, and Steeda fireball shift knob.

"Obviously, the look of this car is somewhat different in looks from most Mustangs – Cobra Rs and Bullitts – and that's exactly the way I wanted it. After all, why be just another face in the crowd!"

Shown here is a prototype version of Kenne Bell's new 1.7L based 2005 Mustang 4.6L SOHC 3-valve modular V-8 engine kit. The sensor wires denote that this is an R&D mule. Although not yet federally certified, the new kit has produced a whopping 460 hp. That's 181 hp over stock!

Kenne Bell also manufactures an air-to-water design intercooler for the 1996-2004 4.6L SOHC 2-valve and 4.6L DOHC 4-valve modular engines. These custom-designed bar-and-plate aluminum-capped intercoolers are capable of reducing the charge temperature between 20 and 30 percent ambient.

Ford mod motors ranging from 1⅞ inches to 4⅛ inches in diameter," says Bell.

Kenne Bell manufactures these pulleys out of machined steel billet (available in 6-, 7-, and 8-rib applications) because with a friction (belt) drive, aluminum pulleys tend to wear faster. Kenne Bell's one-bolt feature also makes them easy to remove. For example, you can change pulleys right there at the track with a simple wrench, a socket, and a breaker bar. However, depending on the diameter of the actual pulley, you may need a shorter serpentine belt.

Intercooling is another way to safely increase horsepower, and Kenne Bell offers an intercooler option with all of their Ford modular-engine supercharger kits. "Our custom-manufactured bar-and-plate designs, air-to-water aluminum intercoolers with custom end caps, are some of the best in the industry. We offer these units for the 1996-2004 4.6L, SOHC 2-valve, and for the 1996-2004 DOHC 4-valve modular engines, and we're currently working on an application for the 2005 3-valve modular engine Mustang."

How effective are these units?

"Typically we can reduce the charge temperature up to 90 percent. The best way to describe it is that it will get the temperature down to 20 to 30 degrees ambient. Aside from the obvious gain in horsepower, an intercooler also represents real value. For example, if you were to install headers, exhaust, and a cold air kit, which represents approximately $1,000 invested, you might gain up to 15 hp at the rear wheels. Our intercooler retails for around $1,200, and is capable of producing 66 hp at the rear wheels. Do the math!"

Although 5.0L Ford small-block owners may be left out in the cold in regard to Kenne Bell intercoolers, the company does offer the larger-sized Flowzilla supercharger inlet manifold as an upgrade over the standard 5.0L/GT40 Kenne Bell supercharger inlet manifold. The GT40-based Flowzilla was designed to complement the larger-displacement 2.2L and 2.4L Blowzilla twin-screw superchargers, producing from 6 to 18 psi. The Flowzilla provides up to a 50 percent increase in airflow, and accepts

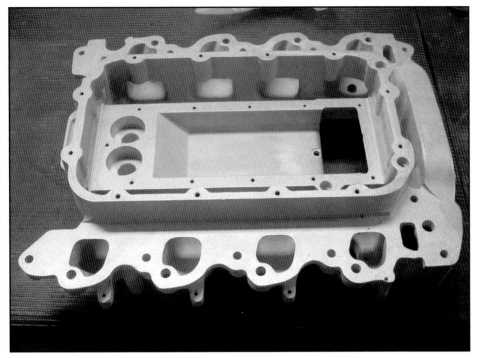

Shown is Kenne Bell's own manufactured 4.6L DOHC 4-valve intercooler intake manifold, which is an integral component in an intercooled Kenne Bell 4.6L Ford modular engine twin-screw supercharger kit.

Allen Engine Development's race-only system for the 4.6L SOHC Mustang and Thunderbird is based around the Lysholm 2300 AX twin-screw supercharger. This kit features Allen Engine Development's Rev I cast-aluminum intake manifold, an air-to-water intercooler system, Bosch electric water pump, twin 58-mm throttle bodies, billet-aluminum fuel rails, and alternator and idler pulley brackets. This kit is reputed to deliver up to 800 hp and 20 psi.

throttle body sizes up to 90 mm. The unit also features an internal bypass valve, and is EGR adaptable.

Kenne Bell's Boost-A-Pumps will deliver 50 percent more fuel and will support 50 percent more horsepower. Boost-A-Pump's fuel flow and line pressure can be regulated with adjustments from 1 percent to 50 percent by the turn of the cockpit-controlled dial, which means you're no longer locked into a fixed flow rating and line pressure setting. You can safely adjust fuel and line pressure for either altitude or for motorsports competition at will.

Kenne Bell's cockpit controlled Boost-A-Spark taps into your existing OE ignition system and is adjustable in increments from 0 to 50 percent. Kenne Bell's Long Spark Technology increases and regulates voltage, far more than short-spark CD systems, and the unit automatically adjusts spark to meet engine requirements.

Kenne Bell also offers recalibrated Switch Chips, boost, temperature, fuel pressure and vacuum gauges, calibrated thermostats, and water injection kits. If it has anything to do with twin-screw supercharger technology, Kenne Bell has it.

Kenne Bell Superchargers
10743 Bell Court
Rancho Cucamonga, CA 91730
Phone: (909) 941-6646
Tech: (909) 941-0985
Fax: (909) 944-4883
www.kennebell.net

Other Twin-Screw Superchargers

Allen Engine Development
2521 Palma Drive
Ventura, CA 93003
Phone: (805) 658-8262
Fax: (805) 658-8645
www.allen@allenengine.com

Ford Racing Performance Parts
44050 Groesbeck Highway
Clinton Township, MI 48036-1108
Phone: (586) 468-1356
www.fordracingparts.com

TWIN-SCREW SUPERCHARGING A CLASSIC

There isn't a classic Mustang owner on the planet who doesn't wish that he or she had more power at their disposal – whether they need it, or not. Call it the human condition, but the fact of the matter is Mustang owners just can't resist extra power!

Of course, you could always go "old school" and add multiple carburetion, a cam, headers, and all the traditional stuff. But then what do you have? A gas-guzzler that's nearly undrivable and most likely a gross polluter, making it the target of every traffic cop in town. "So, what's a mother to do?"

In recent years, quite a few classic Mustang owners have stepped up to the plate and gone with 5.0L EFI power, and have been all the better for it. Such was the case with this black-and-white-striped 1965 Mustang convertible, a.k.a. the *Skunk*. The *Skunk* was actually one of the first classic Mustangs in Southern California to be converted over to 5.0L EFI power all the way back in 1992 by the late Jim Madden and famed 5.0L/4.6L expert Mark Sanchez from Advanced Engineering West (AEW).

Already five times removed from box stock, our 5.0L featured a Ford Motorsport B-303 roller cam, a set of SVO 1.6:1 roller-rocker arms, an SVO cast-aluminum Cobra upper intake plenum and GT40 lower intake, a set of Doug's Headers Tri-Y headers and Magna-Flow mufflers, an Art Carr C-4, and an 8-inch Traction Lok rear end with Currie 3.00:1 gears. Over the years, this combination had managed to keep up with the Camaros and Firebirds, but the *Skunk*'s owner definitely wanted more power!

A supercharger of some type was the answer. However, with space limitations being what they are with an early-model Mustang, deciding exactly what kind of supercharger to use required a little researching. The owner decided on the 1.5L Kenne Bell TS-1500 kit for the

1986-1995 5.0L Mustangs, partially because it was pretty much a straightforward bolt-on proposition.

At that point, we were pretty convinced, but old Jim Bell had some ideas of his own.

"The 1.5L TS-1500 is okay," said Bell. "But I know you well enough to know that you're going to want to eventually hop up that darned thing. What I recommend is that you purchase the base kit, and upgrade the supercharger to one of our 2.2L Blowzilla TS-2200s. Instead of the 6- to 8-pound range delivered by the TS-1500, the 2.2L Blowzilla twin-screw compressor was designed to provide up to 20 pounds max boost."

Bell went on to relate that the 2.2L "Blowzilla" twin-screw supercharger is about 50 percent larger internally, and features a more aggressive lobe design. Blowzilla also features a bypass valve, which bleeds off excess pressure when you're not running at full boost.

"The beauty of this blower is that due to its size, you can run 6 to 8 pounds boost on the street (using the 3⅛-inch pulley) running on unleaded high-octane pump gas. Then whenever you go to the track, you can change out the pulley to something like a 2⅛-inch-diameter drive pulley in less than 10 minutes, time. With 100+ octane gas in the tank, you can run between 17 and 18 pounds boost!"

The 2.2L Kenne Bell Blowzilla twin-screw supercharger also features

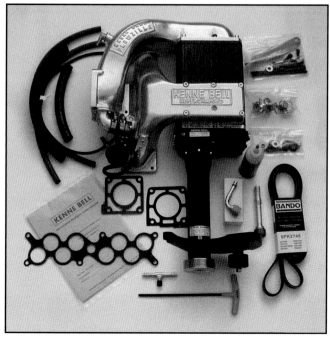

This is an overview of Kenne Bell's 1986-1995 5.0L-based twin-screw supercharger kit for the Fox generation Mustang with 2.2L Blowzilla supercharger upgrade. With 50 percent more capacity, Blowzilla is capable of producing the big (boost) numbers ranging from 8 to 20 psi. This kit is 50-state-emissions-legal.

the Flowzilla air inlet that flows like gangbusters. For this application, we selected one of Accufab's 70-mm polished billet-aluminum throttle bodies with EGR spacer plate, along with one of the company's calibrated throttle position sensors.

Of course, with the bigger blower and more boost, the stock 19-lb/hr stock injectors wouldn't come close to getting the job done. In their place, we substituted a set of Bosch 30-lb/hr units, which, when working in conjunction with our 22-gallon Fuel Safe fuel cell and 230-lph Bosch electric fuel pump, certainly won't be starving our 5.0L for fuel! We also upgraded our mass airflow meter (MAF) to a 90-mm K&N-filtered Kenne Bell MAF (as used on the SVT Lightning) to provide our 5.0L with a bigger gulp of fresh air.

Now that we had the kit, the next step was installing it. Once again, Mark Sanchez and his son Vincent (who as a young boy had helped his father originally install the 5.0L engine in the *Skunk*) were slated to do the work. A mere 4 hours from the moment we pulled through the door, Team AEW had the engine up and running, and ready to deliver to Doug's Headers shop. Once there, Doug and the boys installed a set of his ceramic-coated 1⅝-inch diameter primary Tri-Y headers and a custom-fabricated 2½-inch exhaust including one of Doug's ceramic-coated X-pipes. From there, the spent gases exit through a pair of 4 x 9 x 18-inch Magnaflow stainless-steel mufflers, and out through a pair of 2½-inch ceramic-coated tailpipes. It's a real nice system, and it should help out considerably in the horsepower department.

With our '65 back at AEW, we drove over to Kenne Bell's facility where Dynamometer Technician/Product Engineer Brent Morris was waiting to get with the program. Fuel mapping and overall engine programmings are both important parts of the process. Just prior to dyno testing, engine systems programmer Ken Christley burned a "30-lb chip" (for our 30-lb/hr injectors) and installed it in our computer. Then, with 20 degrees of advance in the distributor and 116-octane Sunoco unleaded in the fuel cell, Morris conducted a series of three pulls, with our best being the second pull, which registered the following data at 12 psi:

308.2 hp at 4,900 rpm and 434.4 ft-lbs of torque at 2,600 rpm

Now that's pretty darned good for a slightly warmed over, 55,000-mile 5.0L small-block. Of course, the most noteworthy gain was in the torque department. We're really going to have our hands full when all 434.4 ft-lbs of torque kick in.

Could we have extracted more horsepower and torque out of our 2.2L Kenne Bell-supercharged early-model Mustang? Yes and no. Actually, we tried to run more boost, but that proved counter productive. Technician Brent

Morris changed out the drive pulley from 3⅛ inches to 2⅞ inches, and the engine started to come alive during the third pull. Unfortunately, the OE ignition system began crapping out and started dropping sparks at high RPM. The addition of an MSD 6BTM electronic ignition set up to retard timing under full boost while controlling detonation would certainly help. And Jim Bell had a few ideas of his own.

"Had this been a stick (due to parasitic loss from the torque converter), we would have realized another 60 horsepower right off the bat. And since this is also a non-lock-up torque converter, you easily lose an additional 30 horsepower throughout the entire power band. Had we been able to regain that lost horsepower, we would have had ourselves close to a 400-horsepower blown Ford small-block!"

So what's in store for this Kenne Bell-supercharged *Skunk*? Well, now that we know what this system is capable of, we're going to build up a fresh small-block using an Authorized Engine Remanufacturing (AER) 5.0L roller cam block as the foundation. After installing another B-303 cam inside, we're going to drop on a set of Holley System Max big-valve aluminum cylinder heads, Extrude Hone the intake, install the MSD 6BTM, and a few other goodies. But for the time being, we're more than happy with what we already have. And really, who wouldn't be?

Sources

Kenne Bell Superchargers
10743 Bell Court
Rancho Cucamonga, CA 91730
Phone: (909) 941-944-6646
Tech Line: (909) 941-0985
Fax: (909) 944-4883
www.kennebell.net

Accufab Engineering
1516 E. Francis Street, Unit A
Ontario, CA 91761
Phone: (909) 930-1751
Fax: (909) 930-1753
Email: Accufab1@aol.com

Advanced Engineering West (AEW)
1516 E. Francis Street, Unit B
Ontario, CA 91761
Phone: (909) 930-9845

Doug's Headers
1391 Dodson Way
Riverside, CA 92507
Phone: (909) 788-4878
Fax: (909) 788-3038
www.dougsheaders.com

MSD Ignition
A Division of Autotronic Controls
   Corp.
1490 Henry Brennan Drive
El Paso, TX 79936
Phone: (915) 857-5200
Fax: (915) 857-3344
www.msdignition.com

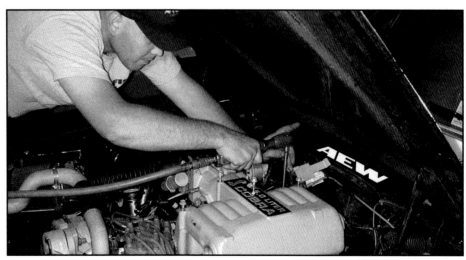

1. Teardown begins by removing a total of four ½ x 6-inch intake bolts that secure the cast-aluminum "Cobra" upper intake plenum to its base.

2. The hose clamps are removed, which secure the air inlet tube to both the MAF and 65-mm throttle body.

3. The throttle linkage cable assembly is removed from the throttle body using a 10-mm socket.

4. After disconnecting the PCV and power brake booster lines, the Cobra cast-aluminum upper intake is removed. This component is NOT reused in the installation.

5. The three 13-mm bolts are removed, which secure the 5.0L's Sanden air-conditioning compressor to the air-conditioning bracket.

6. The air-conditioning compressor bracket is removed after removing a pair of ⁹⁄₁₆-inch bolts and an ¹¹⁄₁₆-inch stud nut, which secures the air-conditioning bracket in place.

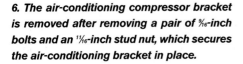

7. Off comes the 5.0L Idle Air Control (IAC) motor from the factory Ford throttle body, which is then reinstalled onto the polished Accufab 70-mm throttle body using the factory ⁵⁄₁₆-inch throttle body mounting bolts.

8. One of the few modifications needed when installing either the Kenne Bell 1.5L or 2.2l twin-screw supercharger is the existing AC compressor bracket. First, our installer marks the area needing to be trimmed using a template provided in the Kenne Bell Blowzilla assembly instructions. Then a die grinder is used to make the cut.

9. Once the bracket has been modified, the AC compressor and bracket get reinstalled onto the engine using the same factory bolts.

10. Now it's time to install the 2.2L Kenne Bell Blowzilla twin-screw supercharger onto the GT40 lower intake. As you can see, this is a two-man job.

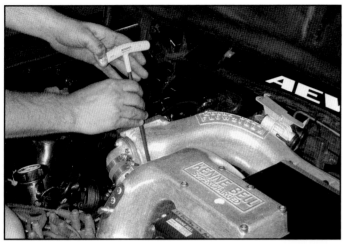

11. *The provided T-handle is used to install the air inlet and discharge tube mounting bolts.*

12. *With the Blowzilla supercharger in place, it's time to final-tighten the factory Ford AC after tightening the Kenne Bell supercharger mounting plate. The provided spacers have been installed.*

13. *With the Kenne Bell supercharger bracket in place, the series of ½-inch bolts are installed, which secure the supercharger mounting-bracket to the front of the 5.0L engine.*

14. *The supercharger mounting bracket shims are fitted. These shims are various sizes because not all 5.0L Ford small-block engines (Mustang, passenger car, truck) are the same.*

15. *Using the provided factory bolts, the Accufab 70-mm throttle body and accompanying linkage is installed.*

16. *The compressor oil reservoir is filled with the oil provided by the manufacturer. Extreme caution is advised. Follow the directions in the Kenne Bell assembly manual to the letter, as over-filling the supercharger damages the unit.*

17. Next comes installing the serpentine blower belt. Installation is made easier by first removing the upper pulley.

18. With Blowzilla almost ready to spin, our installer reconnects the EGR valve line at the back of the supercharger.

19. The breather tube assembly is hooked up, which runs between the valve cover and the EGR spacer plate.

20. The recalibrated Accufab TPS sensor is installed onto the throttle body using the two machine screws provided with the unit.

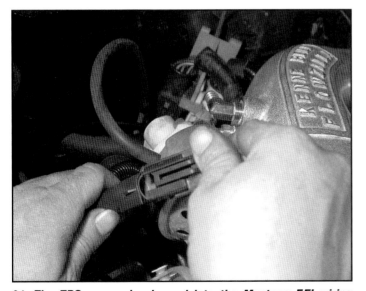

21. The TPS sensor is plugged into the Mustang EFI wiring harness.

22. The air inlet tube is reconnected to the new 70-mm Accufab billet-aluminum throttle body and 90-mm Lightning MAF using the provided hose clamps.

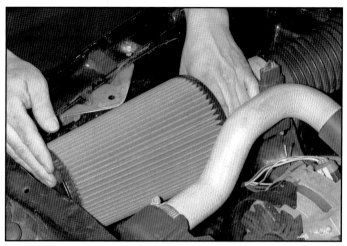

23. And finally, a new K&N Lifetime conical air filter gets installed to ensure that nothing but clean air gets to our Blowzilla-equipped Skunk.

24. After removing the old exhaust system, the passenger-side headers are installed from down below. Note that the gaskets have already been placed on the header flange using Permatex and masking tape; this eases installation.

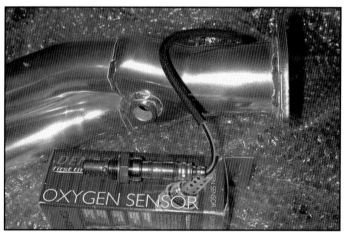

25. In keeping with the fact that this 5.0L is controlled by a Ford EEC IV processor, these headers were modified to accept a pair of ¾-inch NPT threaded header bungs in order to accommodate a pair of Denso 02 sensors, which are an absolute must with an electronically managed V-8 engine.

26. After securing the headers from the underside with a couple of ⁷⁄₁₆-inch header bolts, the remaining bolts are installed, and everything is tightened up.

27. This is the complete ceramic-coated Doug's Headers X-pipe and Magnaflow exhaust system prior to installation.

28. With the headers in place, the 2½-inch crossover pipe is installed using a series of six ⁷⁄₁₆-inch bolts.

29. Next comes installing the Magnaflow stainless-steel mufflers along with the rest of the exhaust system. Then it's time to head back to the dyno shop!

30. The first dyno pull looked pretty promising as our Kenne Bell supercharged 5.0L ragtop registered a best of 307.4 hp running on 98-octane Chevron Supreme unleaded gasoline.

31. Optimistic that there's a little more left in the old girl, the 3⅛-inch blower drive pulley is exchanged for a 2⅞-inch unit, which significantly increased the boost.

CHAPTER 6

TUNING FOR BOOST

Compression Ratios and Supercharging

When matching superchargers to engines, the most important factor to be resolved is the engine's mechanical compression ratio. Since a supercharger can elevate the volume of air ingested by each cylinder beyond that magical 100 percent VE figure – the compression ratio is much higher than it was prior to supercharging – this new dynamic dictates the engine's output and the life expectancy of the engine's suddenly higher stressed internal components.

There's a significant difference in the calculated static compression ratio and the dynamic compression ratio. When you pencil out a static compression ratio, you compare the volume of air the piston's movement will displace with the volume of air that will exist between the piston dome and the combustion chamber surfaces at Top Dead Center (TDC). In supercharged applications, however, the chamber volume will be included in the displaced volume, increasing the Bottom Dead Center (BDC) displacement figure without an associated increase in the TDC volume. This effectively increases the compression ratio, at least under boost.

To optimize a supercharged engine, reducing the static compression ratio will allow higher intake manifold pressure (more boost) without wandering into problems with detonation. Unfortunately, having too low a static ratio can affect drivability. If the vehicle will be expected to negotiate traffic most of the

For an engine to run right, the perfect amount of air and fuel need to ignite at just the right time for things to work out. When adding a supercharger or turbocharger, every one of these parameters needs to be adjusted correctly – or you'll break parts.

time, the static compression ratio must suit those conditions and be high enough to maintain adequate spark plug and combustion chamber temperatures for low-speed operation. This usually requires a compression ratio above 8.0:1.

To allow higher boost levels, the static compression ratio can be set at approximately 7.5:1 with pistons having shorter compression heights than stock. This ratio is useable on the street only if

the engine is exercised on a regular basis. Otherwise, you'll be changing fouled spark plugs a lot more often than you'll care to.

The payoff, however, is awesome performance under boost, which can be raised to at least one atmosphere (15 psi) without worrying about melting your mill. Most high-performance engines with low static compression ratios will handle considerably more than a single atmosphere of boost, but it takes some careful planning to control the spark and fuel demands.

The fuel requirement of a supercharged engine is not precisely related to the increased volume of air under boost. Programming the fuel curve to reflect the increased airflow using the fuel requirements of an unsupercharged engine will result in a very lean mixture under heavy boost. The additional fuel required under heavy boost often calls for an auxiliary fuel pump to control the combustion temperature in the chambers.

While the excess fuel in the engine will absorb large amounts of heat in the process of achieving optimum fuel vaporization, if oxygen no longer remains in the chamber to support combustion, the vaporized (and usually some raw) fuel will leave through the exhaust valve. But without what sounds like a wasteful process, the engine would self-destruct under detonation.

Since the amount of air within the intake tract has been increased, the compression pressure will be higher than normal. The ignition timing must usually be retarded to compensate for the quicker burn time of the dense, rich air/fuel mixture. The entire concept of variable ignition timing is to begin the combustion so that maximum cylinder pressure occurs slightly after the piston passes TDC. Lean mixtures burn more slowly than rich mixtures do, and highly compressed, dense mixtures burn very quickly. The proximity of the fuel molecules with the oxygen in these mixtures ensures fast flame travel.

Blower Cams

It's a given that the more air/fuel (higher VE) you stuff into an engine's combustion chambers, the more exhaust gases will have to come out. Under naturally aspirated situations, the exhaust lobe center on a conventional hydraulic, flat-tappet camshaft has enough duration for the engine to be able to cleanse itself of the exhaust in-between the intake, compression, ignition, and exhaust strokes. However, with a blower, dispensing this exhaust in an efficient

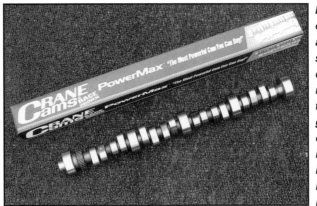

Dual profile cams (blower cams) feature a more aggressive exhaust lobe separation of 114- to 116-degrees duration to allow more time for the cylinder to cleanse itself of exhaust gases. Other notable effects include a reduction in cylinder pressure and increased torque and horsepower through superior exhaust scavenging.

manner using the existing valvetrain components may prove somewhat problematic. To more fully understand the dynamics of camshafts and street supercharging, we spoke with Chas Knight, Domestic Valvetrain Product Manager from Crane Cams.

"When it comes to supercharged street engines, we like to use dual-pattern camshafts wherever possible. Traditionally, the dual-pattern camshaft provides the broadest power and torque band with favorable idle characteristics and good performance. To put it in laymen's terms, what you have with the dual-pattern camshaft is a different profile on the intake lobe master and a different profile on the exhaust lobe master. Traditionally, you have a slightly longer duration lobe (112 to 116 degrees) on the exhaust because of the excess heat and boost that's generated by a supercharger to allow the exhaust valve to stay open longer, remembering that most popular American V-8 engines feature an exhaust port that doesn't flow nearly as good as the intake, and is governed by a smaller diameter exhaust valve. By extending the exhaust lobe duration slightly, it is a very efficient way to increase exhaust port efficiency and relieve back pressure."

What is the best design dual-pattern blower cam? Hydraulic or flat tappet? Roller or non-roller?

"A blower cam can be anything from a hydraulic flat tappet, hydraulic roller, a conventional flat-face solid lifter, or a solid roller. You must remember as a rule, the average street supercharger enthusiast isn't big into high RPM. So, normally for these kinds of applications, you could use a hydraulic

roller camshaft. Of course, with a hydraulic roller camshaft, you can set and forget the valve pre-load once instead of having to go back and readjust the lash intermittently like you would have to do with a solid grind. I guess you could say that it's a more user-friendly camshaft.

"The hydraulic roller cam profiles that are available also provide much more efficient valve motion than you can obtain from a flat-face lifter. With the hydraulic roller cam, you get better idle, better torque, and better horsepower!"

How would you go about selecting the ideal profile blower camshaft?

"This is where it starts to get a little more involved," says Knight. "Normally when you go to a supercharged application, chances are you're going to be lowering your static compression ratio because you don't want to run the risk of constant detonation, or have to run exotic (and oftentimes expensive, and illegal) racing fuel on the street. When lowering your compression ratio to prevent detonation, you'll also need to go to a milder grind camshaft with less

Conventional wet street supercharged systems – like this Holley-equipped, BDS-supercharged, Ford 351W – have long used the traditional 600 to 650 cfm Holley center squirters, which are available in various states of preparation through Holley Performance Parts retailers.

Other approaches to street supercharger induction systems include the use of a conventional "bug catcher," or a two- or four-hole fuel injector housing like those used on the old gasers or dragsters, along with a dry supercharger and digitally controlled electronic fuel injection.

duration on the intake, because you'll now be force-feeding the intake mixture into the engine mechanically. Instead of depending on the vacuum pulses of the intake system to draw fuel into the combustion chambers, you're going to be doing it more positively allowing the supercharger itself to fill the cylinders or do the work."

Prior to delving into turbo cams, we posed a hypothetical, yet commonly asked, question. What kind of camshaft would I use on an 8.5:1 compression, Vortech VS-1A-supercharged 5.0L at 6 psi and 5-speed manual transmission?

"With an application like that we would use a hydraulic roller cam with 226 degrees (duration) at 0.050 inch on the intake, and 232 degrees (duration) at 0.050 inch on the exhaust, with something like a 0.544 to 0.559 (inch) max valve lift. This type of cam would feature a lobe separation up to 114 degrees to reduce overlap so you won't be blowing the intake charge right back out the exhaust."

What type of camshaft would you typically use in a turbocharged application?

"That's another deal altogether. For a basic street-driven small-block Ford application, we would probably recommend a single-pattern grind camshaft where the intake and exhaust would be the same duration, or quite possibly what we call a reverse-pattern cam, where the duration on the exhaust is actually shorter than the intake."

Knight went on to explain that the turbocharger is a thermal pump. It lives on heat, and uses the engine's exhaust to drive itself.

"The more efficient the exhaust system, the more efficient the turbocharger becomes. What you want to do is capture that heat (through a less aggressive, shorter exhaust lobe duration), and use it to drive the turbocharger. With a single-pattern grind, you'll spool up the turbo quicker. You'll get better throttle response. You'll get better power, and less turbo lag.

"Again, your 'average' street turbo-equipped car will be turning 6,500 rpm or less, so a single-pattern hydraulic roller cam will work just fine. Anytime you start getting over 6,500 rpm, you're probably going to be better off with a solid-lifter roller cam application."

Carburetors Versus Fuel Injection

In the long-running dispute over which is the best induction system, the results have generally been favorable for EFI, and in particular sequential electronic fuel injection (SEFI). However, if you're fascinated by things like that (and if you're reading this book, we guess

Many companies make fuel injectors, including AC Delco, Denso, Bosch, Ford Electronics, Hitachi, MSD, and others. Injectors come in two types – saturated circuit (most common for OE applications), and peak and hold driver (used for serious high-performance applications). These injectors are rated in pounds of fuel per hour and are available with flow rates ranging from 19 to 72 lb/hr.

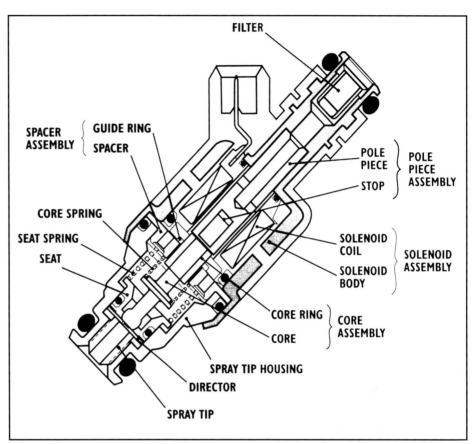

Despite their small size, fuel injectors are very complicated and very precise pieces of equipment. To learn more about injectors and how they work, check out the appropriate section in the latest MSD catalog.

you are), you might be interested in why that is.

The first point for EFI is its amazingly quick response time. The second point isn't as simple, because the tenure of carburetion has been a long and successful one.

Let's cover the importance of response time first. Think about how many events, in terms of fuel delivery and ignition, occur every second while an engine runs. At 6,000 rpm, the crankshaft is turning 100 times per second, the ignition system is charging and discharging 400 times per second, and the fuel-injection system will be timing the pulse length for each of the injectors at the same rate as the ignition system, varying the amount of fuel delivery at intervals of milliseconds to optimize the mixture cylinder by cylinder. That's a darned good trick, by any standard!

A well-tuned carburetor is a wonderfully precise fuel delivery system, but it cannot respond to the requirements of an engine on a cylinder-to-cylinder basis. Instead, the carburetor is dealing with the engine's gross airflow for all eight cylinders. The carburetor responds to a generalized airflow and fuel requirement, where an SEFI system can be

capable of responding to each cylinder as it comes up on the compression stroke.

The fuel injection system is able to control fuel delivery so precisely because it can estimate the amount of time between a cylinder firing and the resultant spent charge passing the oxygen sensor in the exhaust system, for a given engine RPM. No carburetor is capable of that kind of interactive calculation. Typically, fuel injectors are measured in pounds per hour, which is a measure of the actual static flow, or output of the injector. For example, the SEFI system on your average stock 5.0L Mustang V-8 uses a set of 19-lb/hr injectors. Ford engineers decided this was the optimum size to provide the best performance and overall drivability, while meeting stringent emissions requirements. Of course, once you start bolting on big-bore throttle bodies, blowers, etc., all those parameters begin to change. To make more power, you need more fuel, hence, larger fuel injectors.

However, carburetion shouldn't be dismissed entirely. After all, carburetors were the mainstay of the internal combustion engine for close to a century prior to the introduction of EFI.

In one particular instance, however, the carburetor will continue to rule supreme. We're talking about the "carb-in-a-box" setup used on the Paxton-supercharged 289 Shelby GT-350 Mustangs.

Installing a carburetor between the supercharger and the intake manifold eliminates a lot of unnecessary plumbing, gets around most of the problems with pooling fuel in the intake manifold, and presents a more tidy appearance than having the blower draw air through a carburetor. When a carburetor is placed in an air box following the supercharger, it lives (albeit with a few modifications) happily in an environment that changes dramatically as the boost builds. This works well because the carburetor's fuel curve is adjusted relative to the

One of the more popular carburetors for blown Ford small-blocks is a 600 cfm vacuum secondary Holley model for the street, or 600 to 650 cfm Holley Center Squirter for competition use. Shown here is a pair of Paradise Paxton Holley Center Squirters.

And since the system is pressurized, they also need to be equipped with a set of Holley Performance Parts nitrophyl floats, shown on the right.

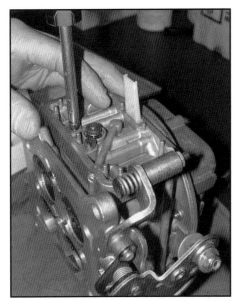

However, these carburetors must be rejetted for blow-through supercharged use.

ambient pressure inside the box. Whenever the boost climbs, the carburetor's circuitry has no clue there has been a change in manifold pressure. All of its air bleeds and the air volume above the carburetor floats see no change in the relative pressure between the ambient and internal systems – therefore, it always thinks its airflow circuitry is at normal pressure.

One more important variable must be considered. The fuel pressure must rise proportionally to the airflow inside the box or the carburetor will lean out under full boost. To accomplish this, you'll need to run a fuel pressure regulator that is variable, using a signal from inside the air box to control the fuel pressure in the same relative manner (relative to boost) as the airflow circuits in the carburetor.

There remains one completely fixed variable in this scenario, and that is the maximum airflow capability of your carburetor. If the carburetor is too small (too few cfm) the engine will run lean at higher boost. For that reason, selecting the right size carburetor is very important to maintain a proper fuel curve. Earlier in this book, you can find airflow curves under various boost levels for all Ford V-8s, and your choice of carburetor(s) should be based on the boost available for your engine in terms of displacement and application.

Keep in mind that airflow ratings assigned to most carburetors are listed at the point where the carburetor will actually start to flag, so your target for selecting a particular carburetor should include a margin of about 10 to 15 percent overage. In other words, if the engine airflow at maximum boost is about 700 cfm, you should select a carburetor with a cfm rating somewhere between 770 and 820 cfm. In most cases, this amount of overage is not sufficient to cause any lag time in normal operation, like a grossly oversized carburetor would.

For a more specific example, Paradise Paxton's Craig Conley recommends a 650- to 750-cfm Holley double pumper to go with his 289/302 Paxton supercharger kits. However, due to the pressurized atmosphere, these units must be specially equipped with larger-size jets, and nitrophyl fuel floats to optimize overall performance.

More good news! Induction systems guru Barry Grant has just released his new Blow Through Mighty Demon carburetor(s) and In-Line Twin carburetors, which are custom-tailored for supercharged applications straight out of the box.

Throttle Bodies

Since most modern EFI systems are either SEFI or bank-to-bank setups, the throttle body is nothing more than an air intake valve that is mechanically governed by the opening and closing of the throttle plate (or in carburetor vernacular, the butterfly). The amount of air required by a particular engine and the way it is equipped determine how big a throttle body it requires.

For example, a stock 1986 to 1994 5.0L Mustang came equipped with (depending on actual year and model) a 60- to 65-mm throttle body. This setup worked just fine with the factory 5.0L Mustang roller cam and 19-lb/hr injectors. However, once you make any high-performance modifications like headers, a more aggressive profile cam, larger fuel injectors, and a freer flowing intake, air requirements go up, calling for a larger throttle body. Thankfully, manufacturers like Accufab, BBK, Central Coast Motorsports, Ford Racing, Edelbrock, Holley, Mac, and Steeda manufacture throttle bodies ranging from 65 mm to a homogeneous 105-mm race bore. Many of these throttle bodies come anodized black or polished, and some even come with fully calibrated throttle position sensors (TPS).

By now you may be thinking, that may be well and good if you're building a conventional supercharged 5.0L, but what about a pure hot-rod application like a 6.71-supercharged 302-W or 351-C?

Up until recently, most GMC-supercharged Ford small-block street engines have used adaptations of classic drag racing fuel injector housings like an Enderle or Hilborn "bug catcher," or two- and four-hole scoop setup, which seems to have worked well enough. However, BDS has just released their purpose-built four-hole throttle plate that looks like a traditional gaser-style four-hole-injector setup, but it works far better.

Ignition Systems

We might be opening up Pandora's box when it comes to aftermarket ignition systems because there are many. The hot-rodder's mainstay has always been the High Energy Ignition (HEI) distributor like an aftermarket ACCEL or Mallory, or even an adapted racing magneto. Either is great for nostalgic appeal, but neither is very good for modern-day street applications.

MSD has made great inroads with their Pro Billet line of electronic distributors, and the company's Programmable Timing Computers, Vari-Curve Controllers, Multi-Function Ignition Con-

trollers, and other products have really changed the street/strip supercharging aftermarket.

MSD's Universal Flying Magnet Crank Trigger Kit for the 289-351W small-block Ford and Ford Crank Trigger Distributor are ideally suited for serious street/strip supercharging and work just great when partnered up with either an ACCEL DFI, Crane Interceptor, F.A.S.T., or Electro-Motive Tech II or Tech III stand-alone engine management system.

Out of all of these units, the F.A.S.T. stand-alone system is probably the most popular electronic engine management system out there. Considered the company's bread-and-butter model, the F.A.S.T. stand-alone system is a standard full-feature, bank-to-bank system. When used with a magnetic crank trigger ignition like an MSD 8640, the F.A.S.T. can be used to control fuel, spark, and ignition (right down to individual cylinders), as well as drive other engine management functions like running your electric fan, electric fuel pump, nitrous, etc.

The F.A.S.T. system is adjustable with any PC laptop computer, and uses true Windows®-based software based on F.A.S.T.'s C-Com-WP software program. Welcome to the world of electronic wizardry!

Barry Grant's new 525-cfm inline twins were designed for the Roots-type blower. The key to these carburetors' incredible performance is that they are "boost referenced." In other words, they sense what kind of load your supercharged Ford small-block is under, and they immediately respond.

Chapter 7

Introduction to Turbocharging

In the interest of practicality, we'll discuss supercharging via a turbocharger compared to a centrifugal supercharger, such as the familiar Paxton or Vortech belt-driven blowers. Rather than being driven with a belt off the crankshaft, a turbocharger's impeller is mounted on a common shaft with a turbine wheel, which is spun by the exhaust gas. Turbos are similar in appearance to a centrifugal supercharger but very different in operation. The turbine wheel must deal with unbelievable temperatures and insane rotational speeds (RPM) even under normal operating conditions.

The efficiency advantages of turbocharging are many, but the biggest is the fact that a turbocharger is almost completely divorced from the engine's overall functionality until it begins producing boost. That fact alone has made the turbocharger the darling of the something-for-nothing set.

If having just another supercharged Mustang isn't for you, take it in a different direction: turbocharge it. Depending on the model/year of your vehicle, someoneprobably offers a single and/or twin turbo kit for your Musang.

Without getting into the ugly calculations required to quantify these powerful little dynamos, the basic difference between your average turbocharger and a centrifugal supercharger is low RPM engine performance. With a crankshaft-driven centrifugal impeller, boost is proportional to RPM. Turbocharger design mandates that exhaust gas volume and flow must be at or above a certain energy level to efficiently drive its turbine wheel before the turbo's compressor will reach a speed sufficient to boost intake tract pressure.

This is very different from the belt-driven supercharger, where the impeller speed is governed entirely by engine RPM and the under/overdrive pulley ratio. With a properly engineered turbocharging system, there's a more flexible relationship between the exhaust energy of the engine and how fast the impeller spins.

The fact that airflow through the two wheels occurs in opposite directions is another fundamental difference between impellers and turbines. The airflow through an impeller begins near its center

and exits the circumference. In the case of the turbine wheel, the exhaust gases first fill a surrounding housing, called a scroll, where they're directed into a curving volume with a diminishing cross sectional area. This accelerates the gases as they interact with the circumference of the turbine wheel. The exhaust exits through the cavities in the turbine wheel, toward the small area near its center. From there, the exhaust flow remainder of the system is normal. This directional difference between impeller and turbine is responsible for their radically different blade or vane shapes, especially their smaller diameters. A turbine wheel is designed to capture as much gas energy as possible, so these wheels feature a more enclosed appearance. An impeller, on the other hand, must be shaped to provide less restriction and freer flowing.

Driving the impeller with an exhaust turbine is a very effective way to do it. The exhaust gases are full of heat energy, but there are other reasons for the efficiency of the system. The first is the presence of a continuous series of very high-energy impulses resulting from – and timed with – the pressure waves exiting each exhaust valve as the engine operates.

Secondly, the generally high speed of exhaust gases provides the pressure to spin the turbine and put the impeller smack dab in the middle of its sweet spot.

Of course, this all presumes that the exhaust gases are applied to the turbine almost immediately after leaving the combustion chambers, before any diffusion or significant temperature loss can occur. That's the tough part in designing a turbocharging system. If you've studied turbo setups that have made it into the win column of any sanctioning body's record books, you've seen that great pains were taken to present the turbine with as much heat as possible, through as little ducting as possible.

It may look like the shape and routing of the exhaust system were relatively unimportant. However, a closer look will reveal that the temperature of the gases takes priority over a streamlined tubing structure.

Exhaust manifolds for turbocharger installations are often surprisingly compact – at least between the cylinder heads and the turbocharger(s). In fact, some of the best Ford small-block turbo systems involve what appears to be a simple (and often surprisingly narrow) tube-like plenum running along the length of each head, with very short connections running to the exhaust ports. The plenum tube is then routed as directly as possible to connect with a similar collector for the other cylinder head, then pointed straight toward the turbo.

As the engine speed approaches the point where its volumetric efficiency is within about 10 percent of its naturally aspirated maximum, the pulses issuing from the exhaust ports are carrying very high amounts of wave energy and speed, which is what the turbine needs. The turbine wheel responds by stepping up its rotational speed and spins the impeller within its preferred range. That's the point when you begin to feel the seat-of-the-pants acceleration that is typical of a turbo, and you know you're in for a great ride.

The time it takes you to get to that sweet spot is called turbo lag. An extremely well matched turbo and engine will have less lag, but it will always be there to some degree. Some of that lag is caused by the need to overcome the inertial mass of the rotor and bring it up to speed. This can be somewhat alleviated by using a smaller-size turbo, perhaps a pair of much smaller turbos, or by making refinements in the exhaust system to intensify the exhaust pulses as much as possible, providing more energy against the turbine wheel.

The last point encompasses the various factors involved in the selection of engine components such as its camshaft(s) and valvetrain components, valve sizes, and port shapes. The actual size or volume of the exhaust system tubing is one of the most crucial decisions to be made, because it must be small enough to avoid diffusing the pulse energy, yet be large enough to accommodate a much higher flow created when your small-block Ford is operating under heavy boost.

Of course, most well-designed street turbocharger systems will also feature a blow-by valve, or wastegate to relieve excess turbo boost, and there isn't a Ford small-block turbocharger application worth its salt that wouldn't directly benefit from the introduction of a heat exchanger or intercooler of some type. Obviously, all of the above makes for a tough balancing "act," and for that reason the street turbocharger industry is more of a "tuner" industry than a commercial bolt-on kit enterprise. Working with a specialist who understands your specific goals is the best approach for most turbocharger enthusiasts.

Turbo Kits and Components

The street turbocharger segment of the automotive performance aftermarket is more of a tuner's niche market than a bolt-on kit market. Just look around and you'll quickly discover that for every small-block Ford street turbocharger kit available (5.0L, 5.8L, or 4.6L), there are at least a good half-dozen centrifugal, twin-screw, and/or Roots-based street supercharger kits available.

But why is this? We thought that we would ask *Full Throttle* TV show co-host Eric Kozeluh, who along with twin brother, Marc, operates Twins Turbo, one of the nation's top small car tuner shops.

"The main reason behind the lack of (although not complete absence of) small-block Ford-based turbo kits is because of the complex nature of the turbocharger versus the easy bolt-on nature of your average street supercharger kit. With a street supercharger you have your headers and you have your exhaust system. All you have to do is bolt one up (supercharger) to your engine, run your oil feed and return lines, and you're good to go!

"A turbocharger is so much more sophisticated a system than a supercharger. For example, you have to fabricate a new exhaust system and new down pipes. And you have to have a proper set of headers built to support the weight and torque curve generated by the turbocharger or the system may crack, and you'll lose crucial boost and power.

"With a turbocharger system, you also need to have a wastegate, or blow-by valve, and an intercooler, which are

The Garrett GT40 turbocharger is factory-rated for engines displacing 3.5L to 5.0L. This turbo is ideal for both V-6 and V-8 small-block Ford applications operating within the 370 to 650 hp range. This cutaway clearly shows the GT40's key components including the compressor housing and compressor wheel (right), turbine housing and turbine wheel (left), and the bearing housing and main shaft (center).

Garrett's quick-spooling GT-45R model is ideal for 4.6L to 8.1L engine displacements. This turbo produces between 600 and 1,200 hp, depending on the engine installation. The "R" connotation stands for "race only."

Shown is an optional polished version of one of the oil-fed Turbonetics/Spearco 62-1 Series premium performance turbochargers, which features a larger-size compressor housing with 4-inch inlet and 2.5-inch scroll. This unit features 10 percent greater airflow than the standard Turbonetics 60-1 models, and can deliver up to 12 psi safely. This turbocharger is ideally suited for 4.6L mod motor Mustang applications.

both essential components to the operation of any well-engineered turbocharger system. You'll also have to have the electronics to control the wastegate along with governing fuel and timing control functions. I guess you could say that while the supercharger lends itself to the backyard kind of mechanic, a turbocharger needs to be set up by a competent automotive technician, and be set up properly!"

With this in mind, where might budding turbocharger converts go to have a competent turbo specialist install a street turbo system on a 260-302, 351W/351-C, or 4.6/5.4L SOHC or DOHC small-block Ford V-8?

There are a number of top-flight turbo specialty shops located throughout the country. Names that immediately come to mind include Innovative Turbo Systems, Bob Norwood Autocraft, Rusty's Total Performance, Texas Turbo, Turbo City, and of course, Twins Turbo. You can also go on the Internet and find any number of competent turbo tuners by logging on to www.turbomustangs.com.

However, all of these shops share one thing in common. They all get most of their domestically manufactured turbos from one of three manufacturers.

Garrett Air Research

First you have the Garrett Air Research "GT" Performance Distribution Network, which features a total of five national distributors for Garrett Air Research Turbochargers and Intercooler products. To locate the nearest Garrett GT Turbo retailer and/or a qualified Garrett GT Turbo installer, log on to www.turbobygarrett.com.

Borg Warner/Air Werks

You also have Borg Warner Turbo Systems Air Werks aftermarket turbocharger program, which like Garrett Air Research's GT Performance Distribution Network, also boasts a complete list of national distributors and dealer/installers. They can be found by logging on to www.turbodriven.com.

Turbonetics/Spearco

Another big player in the street/strip turbocharger game is Turbonetics Turbochargers/Spearco Intercoolers, which is a division of Kelly Aerospace Company. However, unlike Garrett Air Research and Borg Warner's Air Werks aftermarket turbo programs, Turbonetics/Spearco not only sells to dealers and turbo specialty installation shops, they

also sell direct retail. To learn more about these products, you can log on to www.turboneticsinc.com, or you can call the Turbonetics/Spearco technical hot line at (805) 581-0333.

Choosing a Turbo

Of course, there are a myriad of off-shore turbocharger manufacturers with products primarily intended for import applications, and while it's true that some of these turbocharger products may work just fine for your small-block, the reality is you can't beat the product availability, quality, technical support, and warranty offered by the above domestic turbocharger manufacturers. But how do you select the right size turbocharger to suit your specific application?

Obviously, consulting your local installation shop or turbo specialist is always helpful, but at this juncture, you may have yet to choose one. All three turbocharger manufacturing houses offer their own formulas for choosing the right turbo, ranging from complex algebraic equations to handy bar graphs and charts. We'll start with the most complicated and simplify as we progress.

Air Werks K-Series turbos units are capable of delivering between 220 and 430 hp.

Air Werks by Borg Warner

Borg Warner's Air Werks Turbo Systems program offers a formula (and man, do we mean formula) to determine both pressure ratio and the airflow ratio in pounds per minute.

Pressure Ratio

Before calculating the compressor pressure ratio, you must decide what the maximum boost pressure will be (e.g., 7 psi). Then follow this formula:

Pressure Ratio/Atmospheric Pressure = Boost Pressure + Atmospheric Pressure

7 psi + 14.7 psi = 21.7 psi
21.7 psi/14.7 = 1.476 Pressure Ratio

So, we need our turbo to be able to produce about a 1.5 pressure ratio. We'll use this figure in the formula below to find the airflow requirement for our turbo.

Turbocharged Airflow

The following formula is used to calculate the required cfm for 4-cycle engines, which we can then covert to lbs/min. Note! It will be necessary to subtract 0.5 psi from 14.7 psi for each 1,000 feet altitude above sea level to determine approximate atmospheric pressure at those altitudes.

cid x Maximum RPM x VE x DR = cfm

Now let's work through this step by step. To make things easy, let's assume we're talking about a 302. This displacement is divided by 2, (or multi-plied by ½) because the cylinders in a four-cycle engine ingest on every other revolution.

302/2 = 151 ci

You multiply that number by the engine's maximum RPM to get cubic inches of air per minute. Next, you divide this figure by 1,728 to convert cubic inches per minute to cubic feet of air per minute (cfm)

151 ci x 6,000 rpm = 906,000 ci/min / 1,728 ci/cubic feet = 524.3 cfm

However, your average small-block Ford V-8 will only run at 80 percent VE, so you must multiply the cubic feet of air per minute by 0.80.

524.3 cfm x 0.80 = 419.4 cfm

Now you have a figure that represents the naturally aspirated airflow. This figure must be multiplied by the DR rating, or density ratio, to find the turbocharged volume of air. To find the DR, first you must locate the 1.476 pressure ratio (as determined earlier) on the "Pressure Ratio vs. Density Ratio" chart. Now move up to the 70 percent compressor efficiency point, then move left to the DR, which in this case is about 1.25. You would then multiply the DR times the naturally aspirated airflow to arrive at the turbocharged air requirements in cfm.

419.4 cfm x 1.25 = 524.25 cfm

With that accomplished, you can complete the formula by dividing the cfm amount by 14.5 to get the engine lbs/min airflow requirements.

524.25 cfm / 14.5 = 36.1 lbs/min

Using the accompanying compressor map, you can locate the 1.7 pressure ratio line and move across to the 36 lbs/min point. If the point falls between the surge line and choke line, the compressor is a good match. If the lbs/min point falls to the left of the surge line, the compressor could be damaged if used for your application. If the point falls to the right of the choke line, the compressor will be less efficient than desired for your application. As you can see, this compressor is too small for our hypothetical 302.

Borg Warner Air Werks Turbo Systems manufactures a total of 15 different turbocharger models, 7 in their S-Series, which covers diesel engines with horsepower ranges of 100 to 1,600 hp, and 8 in their K-Series, meant for gasoline engines from 140 to 430 hp. Of course, you could always opt for a pair.

Garrett

Garrett Air Research is renowned as one of the world's leading manufacturers of turbochargers for both diesel and gasoline engines. Garrett's line of aftermarket GT Turbochargers is extensive to say the least. Rather than going through complicated mathematical formulas, Garrett has published a handy bar graph that matches turbo size to engine displacement to horsepower rating. By sheer coincidence, Ford small-block V-8 turbo applications fall within the GT40-Series (e.g., GT40, GT40R, GT-42-R, GT-45R) designations, making them quite easy to remember.

Turbo Displacement/hp Range

GT12 .4L-1.2L 50-130 hp
GT15 1.0L-1.6L 100-220 hp
GT20 1.4L-2.0L 140-260 hp
GT22 1.7L-2.2L 160-280 hp
GT25R 1.4L-2.2L 170-250 hp
GT28R 1.6L-2.5L 200-280 hp
GT28RS 1.8L-2.7L 250-320 hp
GT2871R 1.8L-3.0L 300-460 hp

IF ONE IS GOOD, THEN TWO IS BETTER!

This twin-turbo Mustang is street legal and runs 9.90s on the weekends! Like most weekend warriors, Les Iida's 5.0L 1993 Mustang GT started out life 100 percent stock. But with help from friends like Henry Tabios (a well-known island 5.0L racer in his own right), members from the Hawaii Ford Performance Club, Glenn Aarakake and Alan "Naka" Nakamura, Iida's ghost-flamed Mustang three-door has been transformed into a 9-second, twin-turbo terror, recording a best of 9.94 seconds at nearby Hawaii Raceway Park. And, it's still street legal!

"During the lengthy process of building the car (4½ years), there were some considerations. Due to the fact that I have to drive the car to and from the track (25 miles each way), it had to be very streetable!"

Hmm, a 9-second street-legal Mustang? Sounds good to us!

Powering this little gem is a Ford Racing R block, expertly machined by Ted's Machine of Honolulu. The small-block Ford features a SCAT stroker crank, a set of Eagle H-beam connecting rods, Ross 8.2:1 compression pistons with Childs & Albert rings, a Competition Cams solid-lifter roller cam, Clevite engine bearings, a Melling oil pump and Canton 7-quart oil pan, an Edelbrock high-volume reverse-rotation water pump, March pulleys, and a JW balanced flywheel. Bolted up top is a pair of TFS Twisted Wedge R heads outfitted with 2.08-inch intake and 1.60-inch stainless-steel exhaust valves, Competition Cams valvesprings and keepers, ARP head studs, a set of 1.6-ratio FRT roller-rocker arms, and polished Bennett tall-deck aluminum valve covers.

Induction on this beauty consists of a highly polished Edelbrock Victor Jr. intake outfitted with a set of 96-lb/hr MSD fuel injectors. The fun part is the Turbo Technology Inc. twin-turbo kit, which uses a pair of polished Turbonetics T-60 tur-

bochargers pumping out 16 to 20 psi of boost via a Mitsubishi blow-off valve and Turbonetics wastegate. The engine management system, which consists of an MSD crank trigger ignition fired by a F.A.S.T. programmable electronic ignition setup, uses two Windows®-based engine management programs.

Other support hardware on this show-and-go powerhouse includes a set of 1⅝-inch ceramic-coated Turbo Technology shorty headers, dumping into a Craig Iinuma-fabricated 3-inch Magnaflow ceramic-coated exhaust system.

Getting all of that power back to the car's narrowed 3.50:1 geared, 35-splined Currie 9-inch rear end is a Randall Shimodoi-prepared (ACE Transmission) Powerglide with Neal Chance 10-inch, 3,500-rpm stall converter. The final link in the car's power train is a Denny's custom-balanced driveshaft.

The suspension on Iida's GT has been race prepared to accommodate its drivetrain. Aside from the aforementioned Currie Enterprises 9-inch rear end, the car uses D&D tubular A-arms, a Wolf Race Craft front anti-sway bar, and a combination of HAL QA1 coil-overs (out back) and a pair of Lakewood 90/10 struts (up front).

Braking comes in the form of a set of Aero Space four-wheel discs. The Mustang rides on 15 x 3.5-inch Weld Aluma-Star and 15 x 10-inch Weld Aluma-Star wheels with 26 x 15 x 15-inch 275/60 x 15-inch Mickey Thompson tires.

Iida's GT still has its original paint, but it has been flamed in light yellow by artist/painter Dennis Mathuson at Honolulu's Cosmic Airbrush. On the inside, you'll note an NHRA-legal 10-point roll cage, Simpson Safety harnesses, an AutoMeter tach, and an owner-installed custom control panel that governs all systems functions. Other modifications include a JAZ 8-gallon fuel cell and custom battery box installed under the floor pan where the spare tire used to be.

Les and his GT regularly compete in Hawaii Raceway Park's Hawaii's Fastest Street Car Shootout series, and it looks like they do quite well.

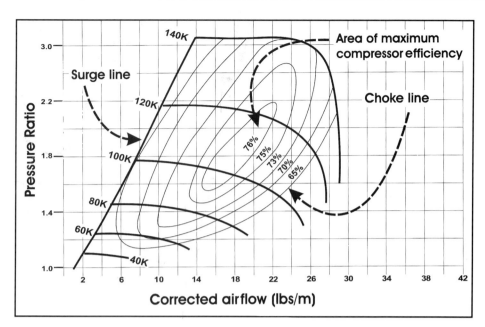

GT3071RWG 1.8L-3.0L 300-460 hp
GT3071R 1.8L-3.0L 300-460 hp
GT30R 2.0L-3.0L 350-500 hp
GT32 2.0L-2.7L 200-420 hp
GT35 2.5L-3.2L 260-510 hp
GT35R 3.0L-4.5L 400-600 hp
GT37 2.8L-3.8L 300-550 hp
GT3782R 3.0L-4.0L 300-550 hp
GT3788R 3.5L-4.8L 400-675 hp
GT40 3.5L-5.0L 370-650 hp
GT40R 2.5L-5.7L 400-700 hp
GT42 4.4L-6.5L 500-1,000 hp
GT42R 4.4L-6.5L 500-1,000 hp
GT45R 4.6L-8.1L 600-1,200 hp
GT60 6.2L-10L 1,450-2,000 hp

Turbonetics/Spearco

Prior to their corporate acquisition and consolidation as divisions of Kelly Aerospace, both Turbonetics and Spearco company's were founded by ex-racers R. A. "Bob" Keller and George Spears, respectively. Therefore, it makes sense that the turbocharger and intercooler conglomerate take a more hands- on approach when it comes to helping the would-be street turbo buyer/installer select exactly the right turbocharger. Rather than complex formulas or graphs, Turbonetics/Spearco cuts to the chase and offers a special Turbo Application Worksheet/Fax Form. To get your hands on one, just contact Turbonetics/Spearco or pick up a copy of their latest catalog.

Turbonetics/Spearco offers a total of 10 different turbochargers, including their

This is a typical example of a liquid-to-air radiator (bottom) along with an air-to-air intercooler (top) Spearco manufactures the items shown here.

T3 and T4, as well as their T3/T4 Hybrid models. Also available is the 60-Series, 60-1 and 62-1, along with their TO4B and TO4E Super Series and their T and Super T-Series models. For racing applications, the company also offers the Y2K-Series and Big Thumper Series turbochargers.

Wastegates & Intercoolers

There isn't a turbocharger system around that doesn't utilize a wastegate. As boost builds, the pressure in the combustion chambers becomes so phenomenal that at a certain point, it can blow out the spark, or worse, break parts. That's why

you need either a mechanical or electrical wastegate to bleed off excess boost. This also allows you to tune your timing and air/fuel ratio based on a consistent maximum boost level. Various manufacturers like ARC, Mitsubishi, and Spearco manufacture these wastegates, and they are worth their weight in gold.

Since turbocharger systems inevitably add heat to the intake charge, an intercooler is a must-have item with any Ford small-block turbo system. Keeping the intake charge relatively cool helps you tune for maximum power while avoiding detonation. There are two popular types of intercoolers on the market. The first is the more compact, air-to-liquid intercooler that has become popular with Roush, Saleen, and Ford SVT on their Eaton-supercharged Mustangs.

The second is the air-to-air design, which is preferred by Ford turbo kit manufacturers like Hellion Power Systems, HP Performance, Pro Turbo, and Turbo Technology, Inc.

One of the drawbacks with liquid-to-air intercooler systems is that you need a coolant reservoir. When it comes to popular street applications like the Ford Mustang that does not appear to be a major issue. Some of your more popular intercooler manufacturers include ARC, Forge Motorsport, Hellion Power Systems, Super Chiller, Spearco, and Garrett.

Of course, the actual temperature drop (roughly 40 to 60 percent ambient) with either design largely depends on the amount of boost you're running and the size of intercooler being used. Quite typically your average street-driven, single-turbo 5.0L/4.6L Mustang can accept up to a 24 x 6 x 3-inch size intercooler without having to move too much around.

The Street Turbo Kit Market

Perhaps the subtitle of this paragraph should have just read, "Mustang Street Turbo Kit Market," because these days, that's where all the action is. Just take a look at all of the discussion taking place at www.turbomustangs.com.

I found four (4) companies that are producing 5.0L and/or 4.6L turbo kits for small-block Ford V-8s. They are detailed below.

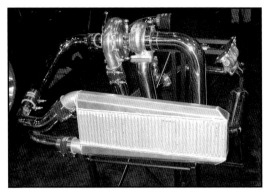

Shown is the Hellion Power Systems new 4.6L intercooled single turbo kit for the 1996-2004 4.6L SOHC Mustang GT. The centerpiece of this kit is a Turbonetics/ Hellion Power Systems 62-1H oil-fed turbocharger, capable of producing up 12 psi.

Turbo Technology Inc. manufactures single turbo kits for Ford small-block pushrod V-8s, as well as a twin turbo race kit for 260–302/5.0L engines based around the Turbonetics 60-1 Series turbochargers. Shown is an example of one of these twin-turbo setups in Les Iida's 10-second street-driven Mustang.

Hellion Power Systems

Hellion Power Systems manufactures intercooled single street turbo systems for 5.0L 1987-1993 Mustangs and 4.6L SOHC 1999-2004 Mustangs. The main pieces of the Hellion turbo kits are the Turbonetics 62-Series turbo, a Mitsubishi 12-psi wastegate, and the Hellion Power Systems intercooler. Dyno tests with Hellion's 4.6L modular-engine kit have produced a best of 430.2 hp at 4,400 rpm and 517 ft-lbs torque at 4,250 rpm.

Hellion Power Systems
2735 Della Road
Albuquerque, NM 87105
Phone: (505) 873-4670
Fax: (505) 880-9758
www.hellionpowersystems.com
Email: john@hellionpowersystems.com

HP Performance

HP Performance offers intercooled street turbo kits for all Mustangs from 1979 to 2004. HP's 5.0L intercooled system, available for 1979 to 1993 and 1994 to 1995 Mustangs, revolves around an in-house-assembled and blueprinted turbocharger essentially built from Garrett components. HP's base package is capable of producing between 7 and 9 psi, but there are optional turbo upgrades for even more boost.

HP also offers a 7- to 9-psi street setup for both the 4.6L SOHC and DOHC Mustangs (1996-2004) centered on Garrett GT40/42 models. Of course, larger turbos are optional. The company also offers an intercooled 2003-2004 4.6L Cobra street turbo kit that is a direct replacement for the factory Eaton supercharger. None of these kits are listed by part number. You must ask for them by name and/or specific application.

HP Performance
301 E. 4th Street
Roswell, NM 88201
Phone: (505) 623-2555
Fax: (505) 622-1451
www.hpturbos.com

Pro Turbo Kits

Pro Turbo Kits offers a wide variety of 5.0L, 5.8L, and 4.6L intercooled single-turbo kits for street/strip Mustangs. Based around the popular Garrett GT40 turbocharger, Pro Turbo Kits offers the following kits:

1987-1995 5.0L Mustang intercooled single-turbo kit, p/n PTKFS-50
1994-1995 5.0L Mustang intercooled single-turbo kit, p/n PTKFS-95
1987-1995 5.8L/351W Mustang intercooled single-turbo kit, p/n PTKFS-58
1996-2004 4.6L SOHC Mustang GT intercooled single-turbo kit, p/n PTKFS-462V
1996-2004 4.6L DOHC Mustang Cobra intercooled single-turbo kit, p/n PTKFS-464V
1996-2002 4.6L DOHC 1,100HP intercooled single-turbo competition kit, p/n PTKFS-464V-T04
2003-2004 SVT Mustang Cobra intercooled single-turbo conversion kit, p/n PTKFS-46COBRA

Entry level, non-intercooled Cost Saver kits and custom-fabricated twin-turbo systems are also available upon request.

Pro Turbo Kits
6630 Topper Run #7
San Antonio, TX 78233
Phone: (210) 657-2706
Fax: (210) 599-4507
www.proturbokits.com

Turbo Technology, Inc.

Turbo Technology is unique in the fact that the company offers intercooled versions of both single (street) and twin-turbo (race) kits. Each of these systems is based around the Turbonetics "60-1" Series turbocharger(s). Listed below are actual applications:

1986-1993 5.0L single-turbo intercooled street kit, p/n 508693-S
1986-1993 5.0L twin-turbo intercooled race kit, p/n 508693-R76
1994-1995 5.0L single-turbo intercooled street kit, p/n 5094955-S
1994-1995 5.0L twin-turbo intercooled race kit, p/n R50TT-1
5.0L/5.8L Big Thumper intercooled race kit, 50RTH
2005 4.6L SOHC 3-Valve twin-turbo intercooled street kit, No p/n yet assigned

Turbo Technology, Inc.
6211 S. Adams
Tacoma, WA 98409
Phone: (253) 475-8319
Fax: (253) 474-7413
www.turbotechnologyinc.com

THE HELLION MOD-MOTOR TURBO MUSTANG

Hellion Power Systems is already known for their no-nonsense, 100 percent bolt-on turbo kits for the 5.0L 1986 to 1993 Mustang. However, their latest effort, a 4.6L turbo kit for the 1996 to 2004 4.6L SOHC Mustang GT may be their crowning achievement.

Just hours before we met up with Hellion Power Systems' John Urist at the 2004 SEMA Show in Las Vegas, Nevada, John and the technicians from Bassani Manufacturing had just completed a prototype system. The system was installed on owner Darryl Bassani's 2000 4.6L, SOHC-equipped Mustang GT, and it received rave revues at SEMA. But how much power does Hellion Power Systems, 4.6L SOHC Mustang mod motor turbo kit actually make? And just as importantly, how easy is it to install?

Post-SEMA dyno tests conducted at Superior Automotive showed the car made 430.2 hp at 4,400 rpm and 517 ft-lbs torque at 4,250 rpm, at 12 psi. Yes, you read it right, 430 hp with a stock 4.6L 2-valve mod motor with safe timing (10-degrees BTDC) and 91 octane!

"We initially wanted to keep this kit simple like our 5.0L pushrod engine turbo kit, but the reality was that with space limitations being what they are with the massive 4.6L mod motors, we *really* had to get creative with the packaging," said Urist.

"That required some re-engineering of the SN-95 Mustang front suspension system itself. For example, in order to achieve the necessary clearance needed to route the ducting from exhaust-to-turbocharger, from turbocharger-to-down-stream exhaust, and from intercooler-to-throttle body, it immediately became obvious that we would first have to replace that bulky factory stamped-steel K-member with something that offered less space restriction.

"In its place, we've substituted a Granatelli Motor Sports tubular front K-member that also utilizes a set of Granatelli tubular front A-arms, a Granatelli coil-over shock conversion kit, and a set of Granatelli camber/castor plates. Since this is such a critical factor in the installation of our system, we have made all of these components part of our kit. These initial modifications are undoubtedly the most labor-intensive parts of the entire turbo system's installation. After that, virtually everything else involved is bolt-on."

Obviously, hardcore mod motor Mustang enthusiasts will immediately pick up on the fact that the Granatelli K-member is considerably lighter than stock. However, that is not the initial intent.

"Functionality (read "more space") is the prime consideration behind the changeover. In reality, the added weight of the Turbonetics 62-1H turbo and other related components basically offsets any serious weight advantage," says Urist.

Now let's get down to the nuts and bolts of the kit.

"Hellion Power Systems' 4.6L SOHC mod motor turbo kit was designed to utilize the stock OE cast-iron exhaust manifolds for ease in installation," says John. "Our kit also features stainless-steel piping (2¼-inch stainless-steel crossover, 3-inch stainless-steel turbocharger entry pipe, and 3-inch stainless-steel down pipe), which splits into a pair of 2½-inch stainless-steel joiner pipes that can either be hooked up to the factory cat-back system, or run 'off-road style.'"

Aside from the aforementioned Granatelli suspension, other key components include the (crankcase) oil-fed Turbonetics 62-1-Series Performance Turbocharger and the Hellion Power Systems intercooler and wastegate.

According to Turbonetics factory literature, "the Turbonetics 62-1-Series turbocharger is a premium street/strip turbocharger for the engine builder looking for that extra edge."

According to John Urist, the 62-1-Series turbo used in their kit was built exclusively for Hellion by Turbonetics, and features a 0.55-ratio polished turbocharger housing and a 0.81-ratio turbine housing with 4-inch inlet and 2.5-inch discharge tube or scroll. It also features a 62-mm compressor wheel and P-trim turbine wheel affixed to a heavy-duty main shaft rotating on a single ball-bearing drive. This unit is extremely durable and unsurpassed in quality. Spool up time is incredibly quick. Unlike other turbocharger ball-bearing housing designs, the Hellion-Turbonetics 62-1-H is totally rebuildable.

The aluminum intercooler measures 24 x 6 x 3 inches and features a pair of tapered-aluminum cooling tanks with 2½-inch inlets and outlets that run from the turbo to the intercooler and from the intercooler to the 75-mm throttle body. This compact unit mounts ahead of the front radiator bulkhead, directly below the Mustang's air-conditioning radiator, thereby taking full advantage of the car's front air intake opening in the bodywork.

In order to successfully install this intercooler and the requisite ducting, it will first be necessary for installers to remove the pliable Mustang front fascia. Compared to replacing a front K-member, this is certainly not a difficult procedure. Basically, everything is "pop on, pop off," via the factory "Christmas tree" fastener method.

"We also use a Mitsubishi 12-psi bypass valve, which is considered to be one of the best on the market, along with a Turbonetics Evolution wastegate, which again are two of the best in the industry.

"This kit also comes with its own fuel system, which includes a set of 42-lb/hr Bosch fuel injectors, a Ford Focus in-tank high-volume electric fuel pump, and a K&N-filtered Granatelli 90-mm MAF. The reason why we include our own fuel system is because aftermarket hard parts (like custom cylinder heads, hot cams, etc.) are so scarce with these (modular engine) cars, we know that we can hit the nail right on the head with our own calibrated fuel system."

Urist was just as quick to point out that it is absolutely *mandatory* that once the kit is installed, the owner *must* take the car to a reputable chassis dyno shop to have the DiabloSport chips reprogrammed (tuned) for the new setup.

"Every computer is different, and every car is different," replied John. "It needs to be done locally on the dyno. With the wide range of altitudes and climates across the country, and with the different grades of fuels available in certain geographic locales, we have found that we cannot include an ideal performance chip to everyone with our kit. It just isn't possible.

"At the present, we do have one option. You can order polished stainless-steel air ducting, which really looks great when you open the hood. At the present, we're looking at federal (emissions) certification. However, at this writing, both this kit and our 5.0L pushrod V-8 turbo kit are for off-road use only!"

Now follow along with us as we show you how to install one of these systems. For the sake of time, and the fact that we're actually performing this installation using Bassani's R&D mule, the Granatelli tubular K-member and related suspension components have already been installed.

1. Setup begins with using a ½-inch wrench to install the #4 AN 90-degree oil feed fitting at the top of the turbocharger. This fitting hooks up to the oil pressure feed line, which runs from the oil filter mount to the turbocharger to provide sufficient lubrication.

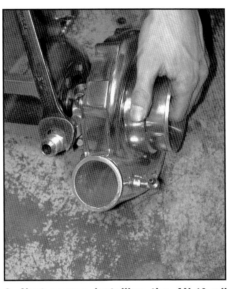

2. Next comes installing the AN-10 oil drain fitting, which is installed to the turbocharger housing using a ⅞-inch wrench.

3. The turbocharger support bracket bolts up to the passenger-side 4.6L 2-valve cylinder head. This is the former location of the air conditioner muffler, which will be relocated and secured to one of the boost pipes later.

4. The turbocharger is then bolted up to the turbocharger support bracket using a series of three ½ x ⁹⁄₁₆-inch factory bolts.

5. Next, a ½-inch wrench is used to hook up the oil pressure feed line to the 90-degree AN fitting at the top of the turbo housing.

6. The oil return line is hooked up, which is eventually connected to an AN fitting at the front of the oil pan using a ⁹⁄₁₆-inch wrench.

7. The provided oil return line punch is used to make a hole at the front of the 4.6L oil pan dead center, approximately 1 inch down from the lip using a hammer.

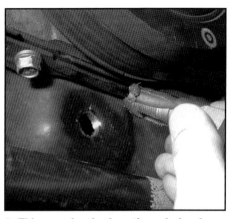

8. This opening is then threaded using a ⅜-inch NPT pipe tap with plenty of grease to catch any metal slivers.

9. A 1-inch wrench is used to tighten the ⅜-inch AN fitting that is being installed into the oil pan. Then the oil return line is attached to the fitting.

10. Here we see our installers laying up the main turbo inlet pipe. The one side is bolted to the stock passenger-side exhaust manifold, while the other end is bolted to the turbocharger.

11. Next comes placement of the steel shim (turbine inlet gasket) between the turbo and inlet pipe.

12. The passenger-side OE oxygen sensor is reinstalled using a ⅞-inch wrench. Since these sensors are so delicate, use a little anti-seize on the threads.

13. A ⁹⁄₁₆-inch socket is used to tighten the turbine inlet bolts to the main turbine inlet pipe.

14. Using a little silicone spray to make the installation easier, the factory air temperature sensor is inserted into the top of the K&N conical air filter, which features its own opening.

15. Installation of the Hellion neoprene rubber 4-inch air inlet tube comes next. One end is attached to the factory MAF, and the other end is attached to the turbocharger, which is secured by a total of four 4-inch hose clamps.

16. The factory MAF plug is reconnected into the new Granatelli Performance 90-mm Mass Airflow Meter.

17. The 3-inch turbocharger down pipe, running from the top of the engine compartment, is secured in place with a 3-inch stainless-steel band clamp.

18. The radiator coolant overflow reservoir, which had been temporarily set aside, is reinstalled.

19. The Turbonetics wastegate is installed onto the turbo inlet pipe and wastegate outlet pipe using the supplied gaskets and ½-inch Allen bolts from the kit.

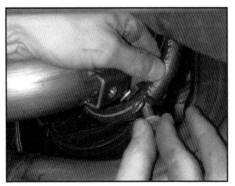

20. The factory AC line is secured to the boost outlet pipe using the factory clamp and a 7/16-inch bolt.

21. A ½-inch and 9/16-inch wrench is used to tighten the boost reference line, which is connected to the turbo scroll outlet and secured to the underside of the wastegate. As boost pressure increases, it opens the waste-gate, limiting the boost to the spring pressure (8 psi). However, in this case it is set at 12 psi.

22. Turbo crossover pipe runs from the driver-side exhaust manifold over to the turbo inlet pipe using a pair of ⁵⁄₁₆-inch bolts.

23. A ⅞-inch wrench is used to install and tighten the passenger-side OE oxygen sensor into the turbo crossover pipe.

24. The 3-inch Torx clamp is installed onto the down pipe, which secures the double barrel exhaust pipe that is routed underneath the Granatelli Performance K-member.

25. Placement of the double barrel pipe comes next. All clamps are left loose for final systems installation and alignment.

26. On the other end of the double barrel pipe, the ⅜-inch Torx clamp that secures the stainless-steel Y-pipe in place is installed.

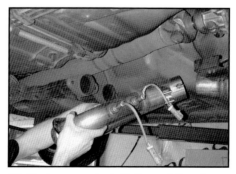

27. Next comes installation of the down-stream-oxygen-sensor-equipped Y-pipe, which slips over the Bassani catalytic converter and connects the forward pipe to the muffler cat-back pipes.

28. A ⁹⁄₁₆-inch socket and ratchet is used to tighten the ⅜-inch bolts and nuts, which secure the Y-pipe to the cat-back system.

29. The two factory downstream O₂ sensors are reinstalled into the Mustang main wiring harness.

30. The stainless-steel Torx clamps (front and rear) are tightened using a ⁹⁄₁₆-inch socket. This secures the exhaust pipe to the forward pipe.

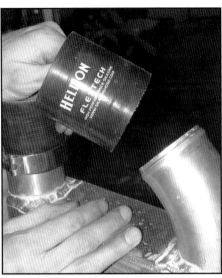

31. The Hellion Power Systems 2½-inch silicone hoses (using the provided hose clamps) are installed onto the intercooler assembly prior to installation.

32. The Hellion Power Systems intercooler is secured to the 2000 Mustang front radiator support bulkhead using a pair of metric bolts.

33. With the intercooler fully installed, the next step is the turbo boost outlet pipe, which runs from the turbo (around the radiator support) into the intercooler using the provided stainless-steel clamp.

34. The intercooler exit pipe (which runs up to the throttle body) is installed using the provided stainless-steel band clamps, and is joined to a 2½-inch silicone hose at the other end.

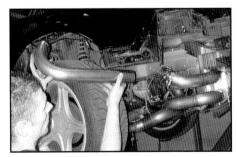

35. The J-bend intercooler pipe sweeps up around the inside fender well and through the opening inside the engine compartment, sliding one end into the 2½-inch silicone hose using a T-bolt clamp to keep everything in place.

36. This is how the Hellion Power Systems intercooler ducting should look when fully installed.

37. *The 2-½-inch connector hose is slid over the receiving end of the J-bend pipe, which is secured in place using another stainless T-bolt clamp.*

38. *The 1⅜-inch silicone hose is slid over the bypass boost pipe, which leads to the throttle body, and is then installed into the car.*

39. *Here's the view a cockroach sees when this turbocharged beast hits the streets. Very impressive!*

40. *With the Hellion Power Systems turbo kit fully installed, it's off to the dyno shop. Here we see Super Automotive's Shawn Ellis burning the first Diablo computer chip as John Urist (left) and Darryl Bassani (center) look on.*

41. *Our first pull yielded a best of 375 hp and 505 ft-lb of torque. Using the initial program, our second pull yielded a somewhat better 395 hp. However, torque didn't change any, remaining at 505 ft-lbs.*

42. *A second Diablo chip, which featured more aggressive timing and fuel systems modifications, is burned. This ultimately yielded a best of 430.2 hp (at 4,400 rpm) and 517 ft-lbs of torque at 4,250 rpm.*